FASHION SALES PROMOTION

The Selling Behind the Selling

Second Edition

FASHION
SALES
PROMOTION

The Selling Behind
the Selling

Pamela M. Phillips

Prentice Hall, Upper Saddle River, New Jersey 07458

Library of Congress Cataloging-in-Publication Data

Phillips, Pamela M.
    Fashion sales promotion : the selling behind the selling /
  Pamela M. Phillips.
        p.   cm.
    Rev. ed. of: Fashion sales promotion / Pamela M. Phillips, Ellye
  Bloom, John D. Mattingly. 1985.
    Includes index.
    ISBN 0-13-362799-3
    1. Advertising—Fashion.   2 Fashion merchandising.   I. Title.
  HF6161.C5P45   1996   95-36919
  687'.068'8—dc20   CIP

Editorial/production supervision: **Janet M. McGillicuddy**
Director of production: **Bruce Johnson**
Manufacturing buyer: **Ed O'Dougherty**
Acquisitions editor: **Elizabeth Sugg**
Marketing manager: **Frank Mortimer, Jr.**
Cover design: **Bruce Kensalaar**
Electronic page make-up: **Janet M. McGillicuddy**

Printed in the United States of America

10   9   8   7   6   5   4   3   2   1

ISBN 0-13-362799-3

Prentice-Hall International (UK) Limited, *London*
Prentice-Hall of Australia Pty. Limited, *Sydney*
Prentice-Hall Canada Inc., *Toronto*
Prentice-Hall Hispanoamericana, S.A., *Mexico*
Prentice-Hall of India Private Limited, *New Delhi*
Prentice-Hall of Japan, Inc., *Tokyo*
Simon & Schuster Asia Pte. Ltd., *Singapore*
Editora Prentice-Hall do Brasil, Ltda., *Rio de Janeiro*

To
Michael Neal Santare
and
In loving memory to
Wendell C. Phillips

CONTENTS

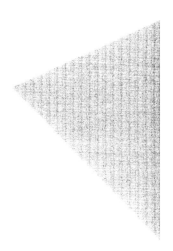

PREFACE

Fashion Sales Promotion: The Selling Behind the Selling addresses those activities that promote and stimulate the sale of fashion goods. It identifies what those activities are, how they are conducted, by whom, and most important, why. It is written for the student of the fashion industry—and for the entrepreneur operating in the industry.

This text gives the reader an introduction to the different areas of sales promotion—and the activities particular to each— and explains how the parts work together to achieve the ultimate goal—retail sales.

Overall themes include the link between sales promotion and merchandising, the vital role of marketing information, and what constitutes effective execution.

Fashion Sales Promotion is designed to be a practical guide to applying the concepts covered. It focuses less on the latest effort of a famous store and more on the concept behind that effort. It is designed so that the reader will apply the most important element of successful fashion sales promotion—creativity—to the study of it.

Acknowledgments

There are many people who contributed their time, expertise, and encouragement during the revision of this book. Special thanks to Eileen Larkin; Thomas Harvin; Jodie Corley, Public Relations, Neiman Marcus; Carol Sharkey, Director of Corporate Communications, Athletic Specialty Division of Woolworth Corp.; Chuck Nugent, Pendleton Woolen Mills; Janet McGillicuddy, Prentice Hall; and Kenneth Santare.

P. M. P.

THE SELLING GAME

Fashion sales cannot occur in a vacuum.

The sale of a product, fashion or otherwise, occurs only when it meets or satisfies a customer's need, want, or desire. For a customer to know that a product meets one of these criteria, communication must take place.

Sales promotion is a form of this communication. All companies, whether producers or sellers of goods and services, engage in some form of sales promotion. Unless a firm can communicate the existence of the product produced or the service offered, no sales can take place. Once there is competition, sales promotion takes on a new dimension and urgency. Now, in addition to communicating information and persuasion to facilitate sales, sales promotion is utilized to convey the benefits of a product or service over like products, the benefit or value of one company over another.

The objective of sales promotion is to sell an idea, product, or service at a profit. Used in the battle for customer patronage, sales promotion arouses the buying impulse by addressing the customer's basic needs, giving the customer reasons to buy, perking interest, and encouraging action. It is used to build customer loyalty, to disseminate information, and to establish or reinforce a company's image.

What This Book Is About

The communication of sales promotion is achieved through advertising, visual merchandising, special events, publicity, and personal selling. Each area has a different role in the total communication effort, but all have a common aim. All sales promotion is selling that promotes a sale of a product, idea, or service. It is this *selling behind the selling* that this book is all about.

Sales promotion aids or promotes the selling of goods and services. To be effective, sales promotion must perform four fundamental tasks. It must

- Attract *attention*
- Generate *interest*
- Create *desire*
- Obtain *action*

The acronym *AIDA,* formed by taking the first letter of each of the words—attention, interest, desire, and action—will aid you in remembering these fundamental tasks. AIDA is the classic model for the approach to selling of all kinds.

Fashion—Another Definition

As a student of retailing, you will come across numerous definitions of fashion. Fashion has been described as excitement, ever-changing fantasy, a form of personal expression, or a display of self-concept. Often it is credited as the reflection of historical and social events.

Yet a common element in all definitions is that fashion mirrors what people are thinking and doing at a given point in time. It is influenced by the way they see themselves and the way they want others to see them, how they spend their days and what they do at night, how they earn their money, and how they spend their leisure time. In other words, fashion mirrors *lifestyle.*

All components of lifestyle must be considered as we discuss fashion sales promotion. Lifestyle is much more than the clothes that people wear; it encompasses our architecture and interior design, our taste in food and entertainment, and the way we spend our time.

An "item" becomes fashion when there are customers for it. More important, an "item" becomes fashion when it sells.

Often, of course, the "item" is apparel. Clothing is the most personal and visible expression of a person's concept of self. We often see the word "fashion" used to mean an article of clothing or an accessory. For example, the bulletin on a magazine cover announcing "Fall Fashions" or an editorial that speaks of "Paris Fashion" is conveying information about the latest in styles of clothing.

For the purpose of this book, and for studying the various elements and execution of fashion sales promotion, it is important for you to remember that fashion sales promotion takes inspiration from all aspects of lifestyle rather than just from clothing trends and style developments. The customer's lifestyle will not only drive what is "fashion," but the communication of sales promotion itself.

Not everyone who buys and wears a particular fashion is involved in the lifestyle from which that fashion grew. The popularity upsurge of active sports apparel was not entirely due to an increased need for functional clothes; active sports apparel is worn by many who do not actually participate in athletics. As popular thinking turned to health and physical fitness, clothes associated with active sports became fashion because people included concepts connected with those sports in their self-image.

A 1994 survey, conducted by Directions for Decisions, Inc. for the Sports Apparel Products Council of the Sporting Goods Manufacturers Association, found that 86% of the U.S. population owns sports apparel, while only 8% of the population actually uses sports apparel strictly for sports or fitness activities.

The survey found that ownership of sports apparel is divided almost equally among men (86%) and women (85%). Interestingly, consumers who do not participate in any sports activities account for 25% of all dollars spent on sports apparel, a $32.2 billion industry at retail. Shattering the stereotype that only women are serious shoppers, the study reports that men spend more each year on sports apparel and shop more frequently than women. Maria Stefan, executive director of the Sporting Goods Manufacturers Association, attributes sports apparel's popularity to several facts: it is physically comfortable and affordable, rarely goes out of style, and gives people a positive image. "Sports apparel confers an image of being fit and belonging to a certain group," says Stefan. "Even if someone is a couch potato who never participates in sports, he/she can be perceived as a runner and a Knick's fan."

The NIKE ad in Figure 1.1 draws upon people's desire to belong to a group, even if it is in image only. There is no "benefits" selling here; the communication does not include reasons why NIKE running shoes are better than other brands of running shoes. "Where your world becomes the next two strides" is accompanied only by the NIKE symbol and the words "NIKE running."

Instead, the message of the ad is one of image. The message is intended for not only those who would actually run in a marathon, but for those who include the dedication and endurance of a marathon runner in their own self-image. The communication of this ad is aimed at the customer who wants be included in a group of people who push themselves to the physical limit.

Reaching Out to the Customer

Stores today carry the same merchandise as their direct competition. Except for slight variations, the merchandise mix of each similar store offers customers the same choice at the same price. What makes the customer choose one store over another?

Presentation is the variable that makes one store stand out from its competition. Through its sales promotion activities, a store conveys its image to the customer. The image may be one of service, price, or the "latest in fashion," depending on the customer the store is trying to reach.

Differences in presentation are achieved not only through advertising, but in the kind of special events the store holds, the way it displays its merchandise, and the image it projects through publicity. We will examine all these aspects of sales promotion and will see how each contributes to the variable of presentation.

Figure 1.1

This NIKE ad for running shoes does not sell the benefits of the product over other brands. Its purpose is to convey an image; its message is intended for a wider audience than just those consumers who run in marathons. Reprinted with permission of NIKE, Inc.

The major driving force behind presentation is the customer the store is attempting to communicate with, to attract, to sell to. To do this successfully, the retailer must know that customer.

A Matter of Survival

Stores depend on sales promotion to build traffic and to make sales. Without sales promotion, a store would have to survive on customers who happened to walk by the door. This method of doing business is possible only under special circumstances. For example, the small retailer in a hotel lobby can feed off the traffic the hotel supplies; prospective customers have to pass by the retailer's front door to get in or out of the building.

Most stores, however, would wither and die if they did not announce to their target customers that they are open and anxious to do business.

The Only Constant: Change

Operating a healthy retail business is not an easy task. There are many factors that make the retailer's job—selling goods and services to the consumer for a profit—very tough.

Some of these factors are external conditions. These affect the business climate in general and affect retailers and their customers directly. External conditions include the economic climate, retail competition, and the makeup of the market in which the retailer operates.

Fluctuating factors such as inflation rates, unemployment rates, interest rates, and the cost of essential items such as housing and food all affect the fashion retailer. Wait a minute—what have those boring statistics to do with fashion sales promotion? While boring, those rates and stats nevertheless directly affect the *consumer's* buying power. Simply put, those factors cut into the amount of consumer *discretionary income,* that is, money left over after the essentials are paid for. And that directly affects the fashion retailer.

Stiff competition is another external factor challenging retailers. More and more stores are competing for the same consumer dollars, with similar merchandise, in the same retail markets, at the same price. Just as Lord & Taylor has moved west to capture new markets, Neiman Marcus has moved east.

The actual size and makeup of the market in which a retailer operates is affected by social factors. The statistical study of the human population is the study of demographics—the identification of the population by numbers of people and measurable attributes of that population.

Shifting demographics drain customers from one trading area while increasing the number of customers in another. It could be a trend of people moving from the city into suburban areas or it could be a population shift into a geographic zone, such as into the Sunbelt in the United States. If, for example, the population soars in states like Texas, Arizona, and California, it is logical to assume that retail customers are being drained from other sections of the nation.

In addition, the overall makeup of the population continually changes. This information is important to the retailer because significant changes, such as a drop or an increase in the birthrate, or a general trend toward increased longevity, influence the type of goods needed by the consuming public. Similarly, trends such as an increased percentage of women returning to the work force after the birth of a child or an increased interest in active sports affects not only the merchandise the retailer can successfully market, but the nature of the communication of the successful sales promotion effort.

Unemployment is another external factor that affects the retailer. If the locale's major employer, such as a automobile factory, closes its doors, the economic structure on which a retailer depends is shattered.

The fashion retailer is also faced with price slashing from direct competition. When sales slump, retailers must run specials to move merchandise. If a store's direct competitor marks down a brand name that the store has in stock, it has no choice but to mark down the merchandise or lose customers to the competition.

Internal conditions also challenge retail operations. The cost of doing business, from electricity to shopping bags, from the cost of the merchandise to the cost of health benefits for the retailer's employees, all affect the retailer's bottom line and profitability.

By now, this all sounds pretty bleak, and you are considering a career change. But the excitement and challenge of fashion sales promotion is derived from contributing to a retail operation's success in spite of a climate of constant change and obstacles. However, money budgeted for this area must be wisely and productively spent if the retailer is to realize a profit and remain alive.

Levels of Selling

There are several levels of selling in the fashion industry. The firms involved sell and promote to their customers and to the ultimate consumer. By dividing the market into three segments, as illustrated in Figure 1.2, we can examine the selling and sales promotion that occur in each.

The first segment is comprised of the producers of raw materials. This includes the fiber producer, the textile manufacturer, and the maker of linings, interfacing, trimmings, and other like components of the finished product.

The first segment sells its products to the second segment—the apparel manufacturers. The producers at this level, also referred to as wholesalers, manufacture the finished product.

The second segment then sells the finished product to the retailer. The retailer functions as a dealer or distributor of the finished product to the ultimate consumer.

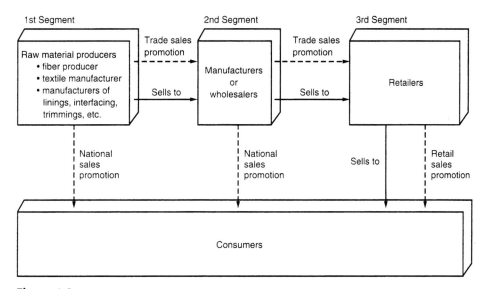

Figure 1.2

By dividing the fashion market into three segments, we can see the flow of selling and sales promotion.

Who Sells to Whom

The sales promotion conducted in the fashion industry can be divided into three categories: trade, retail, and national. Trade selling occurs within the industry. It does not involve the consumer.

Trade sales promotion occurs, for example, when a fiber producer promotes the benefits of its product to its customer, the apparel manufacturer. It also occurs when the fiber producer promotes to the retailer, its customer's customer.

The activities the apparel manufacturer engages in to promote the sale of its products to the retailer are also called trade sales promotion. The advertising conducted at this level is called trade advertising.

Publications like Fairchild's *Women's Wear Daily*, the National Retail Federation's *STORES*, and Lebhar-Friedman's *Chain Store Age*, to name a few, are the vehicles for trade advertising. People in the fashion business, not the ultimate consumer, are the targeted audience for these publications.

The sales promotion activities the retailer engages in are called *retail sales promotion*. This sales promotion is aimed directly at the ultimate consumer.

Retailers are not the only ones in the market who direct their promotions at the consumer. The firms in the first two tiers also communicate the benefits of their products to the consumer. This activity is called *national sales promotion*, and the advertising involved is called national advertising.

The term "national" in this case does not necessarily describe the geographical extent of the promotion. National sales promotion could be aimed at consumers in one city or locale. In this instance, "national" is used to describe the promotions conducted by the first two segments, the producers of raw materials and the wholesalers, when the promotion is aimed at the consumer.

Pendleton's national ad in Figure 1.3 is aimed at the ultimate customer. The ad appeared in *The New Yorker, Bon Appetit, Harper's Bazaar,* and *Self,* all of which are consumer magazines. The ad lists the company's telephone number in case interested consumers can't find the product. When receiving such a call, Pendleton would tell the consumer which stores in the consumer's immediate market area carry the merchandise.

The Crown ad, in Figure 1.4, uses humor in both the copy and artwork to educate the consumer about interfacing in general and Crown's interfacing in particular. This ad appeared in *The New York Times'* Sunday supplement magazine—*Fashion of The Times.* Since many consumers are unaware of the role interfacing plays in the construction of a garment, much less the differences quality interfacing can make, the ad serves to create a demand for Crown's interfacing through its informative copy.

This example of national advertising is unique in that it is, subtly, also trade advertising. *Fashions of The Times* is widely ready by retailers and manufacturers. The ad also informs these two segments of the fashion market about interfacing and perhaps encourages them to rethink their buying choices.

Knowing that his or her customers are aware of the role interfacing plays in the wearability and life of a garment, the buyer may be prompted to question the manufacturer about the interfacing used before placing an order. The ad could also influence the manufacturer to rationalize that the slightly higher cost of Crown's interfacing could be more than offset by the goodwill generated at the retail and consumer levels. Thus, through its national ad, Crown has created demand in all the segments of the fashion market for its product.

The Presell Campaigns

When a producer of raw materials or an apparel manufacturer engages in sales promotion directed at the consumer, he is *preselling* his merchandise. The aim of national sales promotion is to create a demand at the consumer level for brand names.

In national advertising the fiber producer urges the customer to "Buy Brand-Name-Apparel made of My-Brand-Name-Fiber at leading stores." The apparel manufacturer is saying to the customer, "Buy My-Brand-Name-Product at your store."

The amount of presell increases as the competition for a particular product intensifies. By employing national advertising, the manufacturer hopes to create enough customer demand for its product to literally force the retailer to carry it. If the presell of a product is successful, a retailer fears its customers will go elsewhere to purchase the product, and offers it.

Figure 1.3

Manufacturers conduct national sales promotion to presell their products and to create brand awareness. Courtesy of Pendleton.

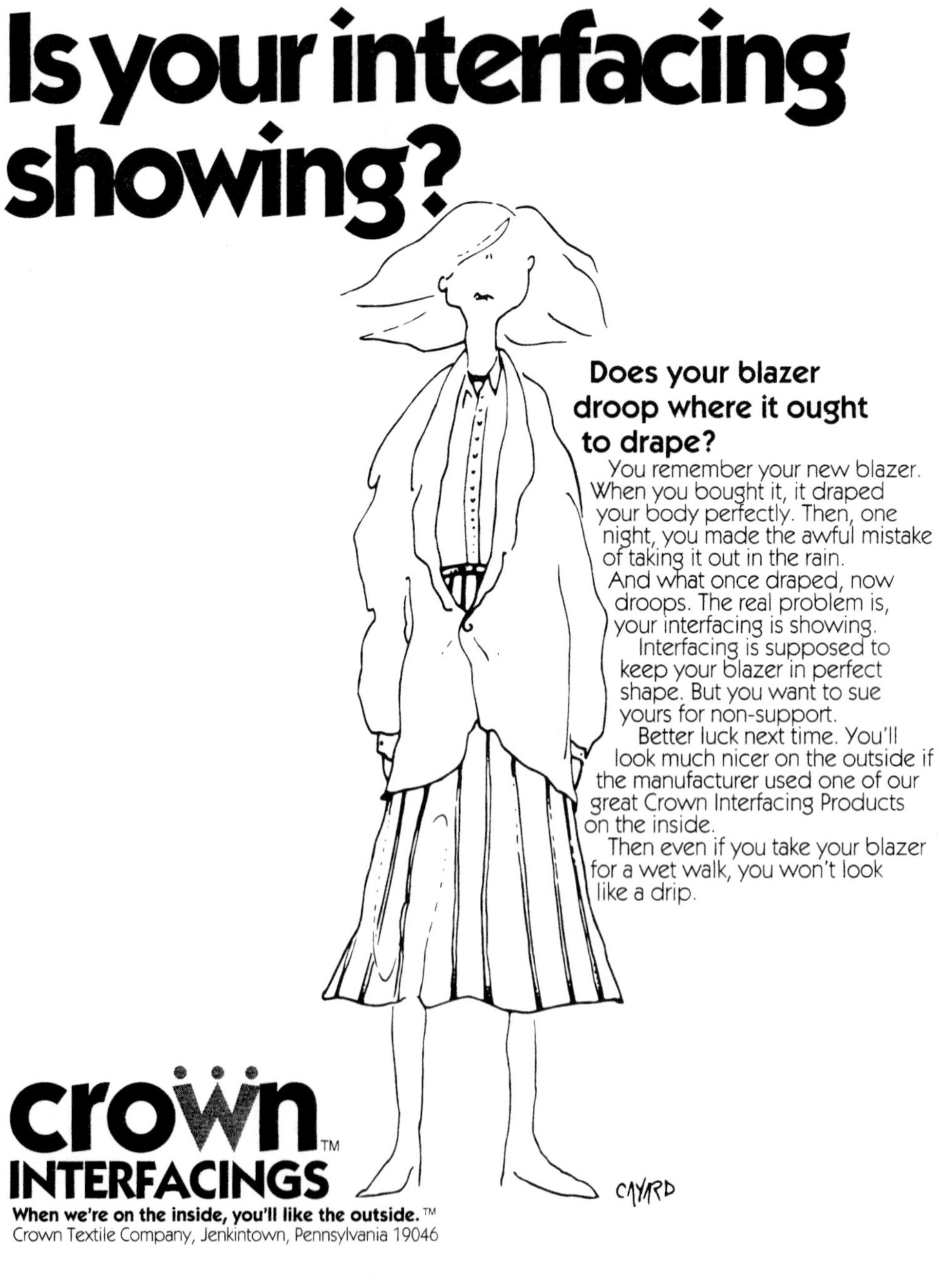

Is your interfacing showing?

Does your blazer droop where it ought to drape?

You remember your new blazer. When you bought it, it draped your body perfectly. Then, one night, you made the awful mistake of taking it out in the rain.

And what once draped, now droops. The real problem is, your interfacing is showing.

Interfacing is supposed to keep your blazer in perfect shape. But you want to sue yours for non-support.

Better luck next time. You'll look much nicer on the outside if the manufacturer used one of our great Crown Interfacing Products on the inside.

Then even if you take your blazer for a wet walk, you won't look like a drip.

CAYARD

crown™
INTERFACINGS
When we're on the inside, you'll like the outside. ™
Crown Textile Company, Jenkintown, Pennsylvania 19046

Figure 1.4

This national ad educates the consumer about interfacing and increases the demand for the sponsor's product. Crown Textile Company, Jenkintown, Pa.; Agency—Altman, Stroller, Weiss.

Additionally, the retailer sees national advertising as a plus. National advertising creates consumer awareness of the product, an advantage for the retailer since the consumer is already educated about its benefits. The NIKE ad in Figure 1.1 is an example of national advertising that presells that company's product. When the retailer runs an ad that features NIKE running shoes, the customer already has been presold on the image/benefits of the product.

Historically, manufacturers left most of the sales promotion up to the discretion of the retailer. The manufacturer offered co-op money, markdown money, and other incentives that will be covered in later chapters, but the decision about sales promotion exposure, how much and when, was left in the hands of the retailer.

In advertising jargon, this is called *push-through*. The retailer was sold a product and had the responsibility to drum up business for it.

Utilizing a method known in advertising circles as *pull-through*, fashion manufacturers are increasingly advertising directly to the consumer, and thus creating demand for their products and brands at the consumer level. This method had been used successfully in packaged goods for some time and, although expensive, has proved successful for marketers in the fashion industry.

The two graphics in Figure 1.5 compare the two approaches. You will note that in the case of the push-through method, the communication is between the retailer and the consumer. The sales promotion efforts of the retailer create the consumer demand. In the second graphic in Figure 1.5, the communication is conducted by the manufacturer to the consumer through national advertising. The demand is then twofold: the consumer wants the product, so the demand is increased at the retail level, thereby increasing sales at the manufacturer level.

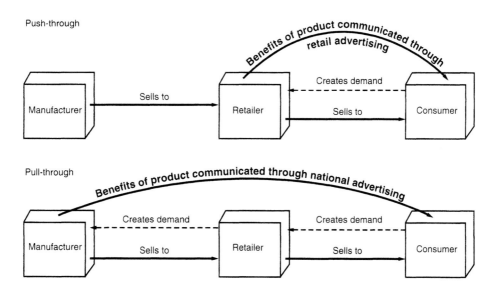

Figure 1.5
Push-through and pull-through comparison chart.

The retailer may also conduct sales promotion efforts when pull-through advertising is conducted by the manufacturer. In fact, many retailers view additional sales promotion dollars dedicated to a nationally advertised product as money well spent. The rational is simple. The retail sales promotion dollar goes further because the consumer has already heard the message through the national advertising.

While the pull-through technique helps the retailer because it presells the consumer, not all products are right for the store. Considerations of store image and the store's targeted customer must be taken into account before the retailer decides to carry a product. In other words, the retailer cannot be intimidated into carrying a product only because the manufacturer conducts an aggressive ad campaign; the consumers who are being presold may not be the store's customers at all.

Summary

For the purpose of this book, we are adding to other definitions of fashion to define fashion as that which mirrors lifestyle. While clothing is the most common and visible expression of lifestyle, other lifestyle aspects—architecture; interior decoration; and preferences in food, entertainment, and leisure activities—are included in our definition of fashion.

Since retailers offer the same merchandise as their direct competition, presentation is the variable that makes one store stand out from another. Through each of its sales promotion activities, the retailer conveys the stores image and communicates with the targeted store customer.

Sales promotion is also important for a retailer's survival. Except for rare circumstances, a retailer cannot survive on the business of "chance" customers; the more people a retailer communicates with and attracts in the door, the better the chances for a profitable operation.

Hoping to create demand for their products, other segments of the fashion market communicate with the consumer. The amounts of presell increases as the competition to sell a particular product intensifies.

Terms for Review

1. Sales promotion
2. AIDA
3. Lifestyle
4. Presentation
5. Consumer
6. Discretionary income
7. Shifting demographics
8. Trade sales promotion
9. Retail sales promotion
10. National sales promotion
11. Presell
12. Push-through
13. Pull-through

Study Review Questions

1. Why is AIDA applied to all selling efforts? How does this acronym apply to retail sales promotion?
2. What is sales promotion and what does it accomplish?
3. What is meant by the phrase "fashion mirrors lifestyle"?
4. Why is presentation important to a retailer?
5. Name a retailer in your area that depends on walk-by traffic. Is this retailer able to survive solely on walk-by traffic?
6. Name two external conditions that are currently affected retailers in your market area.
7. What are the three levels of selling in the fashion industry? Name a company from each.
8. Why do the first two segments of the fashion industry engage in national sales promotion?
9. Explain the difference between push-through and pull-through advertising.

Case

Choose a fashion retailer, either where you live or where you attend school, and create a profile of that retailer. Describe the merchandise the retailer carries, where the retailer is located, what surrounds the retail establishment, and how it is accessed, for example, via foot traffic, vehicle traffic, or mass transit.

Questions

1. What economic factors are currently affecting the retailer?
2. Have there been any major changes in the market in which the retailer operates that would affect the retailer's business?
3. Does the pull-through method of national advertising affect the retailer?

MARKETING

A look at marketing and its role in retail operations is crucial to the study of fashion sales promotion because marketing, and the decisions reached because of it, direct the sales promotion activities conducted by a retailer. Marketing also supplies vital information to the retailer for merchandising decisions.

The need for marketing information increases as the distance between the decision makers and the customers they are trying to reach widens. A retailer who owns and operates a small business—a newsstand, for instance—is in a better position to know what customers want. If the retailer receives several requests for a certain publication, he or she may decide to offer that publication. If the retailer notices a change in the traffic that passes the newsstand—from, let's say, all male executives to a mixture of male and female executives—he or she can adjust the stand's offerings accordingly. The important factor is that the retailer talks to, sees, and listens to the customers who make the purchases.

The concept of the marketing function is not new. Its value has long been proven by manufacturers like Procter & Gamble and General Electric. These consumer goods companies have long used marketing research and test marketing to develop and introduce new products. Nor is the concept new to retailing. In 1916, 18 major department stores, among them Filene's, F. & R. Lazarus, Rike-Kumler, J. L. Hudson, Dayton, L. S. Ayres, The Emporium, B. Forman, and Joseph Horne, formed the Retail Research Association. The purpose of the group was to scientifically study problems of marketing and operations in order to cut costs and operate more efficiently.

Over the years, growing retail competition within a trading area and retailers' expansion into new trading areas have increased the need for marketing information. The goal of any retailer is to meet the needs of the market and to build the store's position in that market. The truly successful retailer not only satisfies customers' needs, but anticipates them.

Some major retailers have a marketing director who reports directly to the chief executive officer. Others give the marketing responsibility to the vice president responsible for sales promotion. In the small retail operation, the job is just one more the owner-operator performs.

No matter what the title, the marketing person in a retail operation acts as store navigator. His or her job: to put the store on course. By monitoring underlying socioeconomic and psychological forces within a trading area, the marketer helps position the store's merchandise, services, and image to attract and hold buying audiences.

A Basic Definition—An Outward Look

The *marketing concept* is an outward look. It is the formulation of merchandising and sales promotion programs in response to the external market rather than to internal performance or resource consideration. It is true that for any successful retail operation the correct balance between merchandise stocks, sales, profit margin, and expenses must be maintained. The resource factor—what manufacturers are producing, at what price—also influences what the retailer offers. But arguably the most important factor—the retailer's customer—must be understood or "known" for the retailer to be successful. It is the customer that drives not only what the retailer offers for sale, but the sales promotion—or communication—effort.

Marketing provides a systematic approach to understanding the climate in which a retailer operates, the retailer's competition, the economic factors that will affect sales, and the consumer that retailer hopes to sell to.

Imagine for a moment the "birth" of a retailer in a developing town in the Old West. The first settlers are primarily men; the need—tools of survival. As the town grows, and more women and children join the growing population, quality of life needs begin to emerge. Now our retailer would add to the merchandise offering: perhaps cloth for curtains and clothing, some ready-to-wear items, and luxury items such as candy. At each stage of the retailer's growth and development the merchandise mix reflects what the store's customers need and want. Of course, our successful Old West retailer has a great advantage over today's retailer. The owner is acquainted with each and every customer, sees them, talks to them, knows how they spend their time.

Today, marketing is used to measure the consumer. Market research discovers who the consumer is, and what are the consumer's needs and wants. Obviously, it is impossible for a retailer to measure each and every customer in the trading area. The alternative is to measure consumers in groups, or segments of groups, to better understand and predict what goods and services can be profitably marketed to them.

There are two types of measurements employed by the marketing function: *demographics* and *psychographics*. Demographics is the statistical study of human population, a compilation of figures describing vital statistics, population size, density, and distribution. Psychographics profiles individual traits and habits.

Utilizing the information supplied by each, the marketing person is able to formulate short- and long-term plans and forecasts for the store. He or she identifies the customer target group the store seeks to reach and charts the proper course for the retailer.

The type of information generated by each type of measurement is as follows:

Demographics

- Age
- Level of education
- Sex
- Race
- Social class
  - Income
  - Memberships
  - Occupation
- Type of residence
- Martial status

Psychographics

- Lifestyles
- Interest in activities (hobbies, sports, etc.)
- Patterns of usage
- Status and price consciousness
- Career mobility

SHOPPER SEGMENTATION

To understand customers' attitudes and purchasing motivations, marketers segment shoppers into groups based on their basic shopping and fashion viewpoints. Shopper segmentation is a foundation upon which marketing strategy is built.

The process of segmenting a market's shoppers into groups is an extension of the method utilized by social researchers. Whereas social researchers group individuals according to their social values and lifestyles, shopper segmentation translates social attitudes and behavior into corresponding shopping attitudes and purchasing behavior.

Changes in social values and attitudes influence people's behavior. These changes affect purchasing behavior: what a person buys and how much the person is willing to spend.

As with all grouping efforts, shopper segmentation reflects the average. There are, of course, exceptions to every rule. But by identifying the characteristics, attitudes, and behavior patterns of their customers, retailers can better position their merchandising and promotional efforts.

PROFILES OF SHOPPER GROUPS

Conservative.   Embracing traditional social values, the Conservatives tend to have a settled lifestyle. Economic circumstances and an outlook that does not focus on apparel as a means of self-expression orients this group toward functional clothes rather than fashion apparel. Therefore, purchases are based on need rather than impulse and are replacement oriented. Primary considerations for Conservatives' purchases center on price, durability, and quality.

Moderate.   For this group, fashion means making sure they do not stand out as being different. Moderates have a functional shopping orientation and purchase apparel only after a trend is firmly established. A budget-conscious group, Moderates enjoy shopping and like to browse in search of bargains.

Consumer Group	*Purchasing Motivation*	*Major Purchasing Considerations*
Conservative	Make purchases based on needs rather than impulse —replacement oriented	Price, durability, and quality are important.
Moderate	Purchase apparel only after trend is firmly established.	As bargain hunters, like to browse the stores.
Classic	View purchases as an investment, not a fashion statement.	Purchases are planned— focus is on quality; store loyalty is strong.
Young Contemporary	As emulators, fashion is a means of self-expression	Quality is of little importance—shopping is enjoyable; impulse buying is common.
Update	Experiment with fashion, blending classic styles with advanced fashion looks.	Fashion appropriateness outranks price and quality considerations.
Trendy	Clothes are used to attract attention—draw inspiration from pop culture.	Shock value of apparel is more important than price or quality.
Advanced	Use merchandise to express viewpoints, make fashion statement—have desire and confidence to assemble new looks.	Impulse shoppers—price and quality are a status consideration.

Classic. Viewing apparel purchases as an investment rather than a fashion statement, Classic shoppers evidence strong self-awareness and definite viewpoints. They are willing to pay more and go to some trouble to find the understated, tailored look that best typifies their self-image. This group is most responsive to service and exhibits strong store loyalty. Most Classic shoppers have a moderate rate of purchase activity, plan their purchases, and show little interest in sale merchandise.

Young Contemporary. Fashion emulation rather than leadership distinguishes the Young Contemporary from other shopper groups. Fashion standards are set by personalities accorded recognition by peers. Clothes are an important means of self-expression for Young Contemporaries, who are not only aware of latest fashion trends, but wish to be the first associated with them. Quality is of little importance, since apparel is never worn for long. This group is characterized by enthusiasm for shopping, browsing, and impulse buying.

Update. Updates exhibit a willingness to experiment with apparel, and do so by blending classic styles with more advanced forward fashion. They seek apparel that expresses their individuality and is functional for their active lifestyles. Fashion appropriateness outranks price and quality considerations. Due to an upscale demographic profile and high rate of purchase activity, Updates are assigned a high economic value by retailers.

Trendy. This is the extremist shopping group; they gravitate toward the radical side of prevailing fashion. Using clothes as a means of gaining attention, Trendy shoppers are constantly on the prowl for newness and find inspiration in pop culture. Price and quality take a back seat to the shock value of apparel items.

Advanced. The prime purchasing consideration of the Advanced shopper group is the ability of merchandise items to make the desired fashion statement. This group represents the market's fashion pacesetters and exhibits the most forward fashion attitudes. A youthful and affluent group, Advanced shippers have the confidence and desire to assemble and introduce new looks. Impulsive shoppers, they see apparel as a means of expressing their viewpoint.

Clarifying the Merchandising Picture

To illustrate the value of marketing information, let us pretend that you have just become the buyer of junior ready-to-wear at Anyplace Department Stores. As one of your first tasks, management has asked that you prepare an analysis of your area and determine what sales increases can be expected.

You begin your research by looking at store records. As in Table 2.1, you note that junior ready-to-wear constitutes 25% of Anyplace Department Stores' total

Table 2.1   Sales Figures for Anyplace Department Stores (Sales in 000s)

	Total Ready-to-Wear Sales	Junior Ready-to-Wear Sales	Junior % of R-T-W
Flagship	$14,775	$ 3,620	24.5
Branch #1	11,720	2,930	25
Branch #2	8,525	1,705	20
Branch #3	9,980	2,994	30
	$45,000	$11,249	25

ready-to-wear business. The records indicate that the most profitable junior department is in the Flagship store, with sales over $3 million. However, you note that the junior ready-to-wear department in the Flagship store contributed only 24.5% of that unit's total ready-to-wear sales. The junior department in Branch #3, while showing fewer sales, contributed 30% of that unit's ready-to-wear business—the highest junior-to-total relationship.

Utilizing a pure *merchandising approach,* you decide that 30% is a reasonable standard for all the junior departments to contribute to the total ready-to-wear sales at each store. After all, you reason, each department contains the same merchandise mix—the same sizes and colors from the same manufacturers. Using the standard of 30%, you come up with the potential sales for each unit (Table 2.2). By subtracting the actual sales for each unit from the potential sales, you see the unrealized opportunity for each department. Since Branch #3 is already at 30% of the total ready-to-wear business, actual and potential sales are the same.

Now that you have a sales increase goal of $813,000 at the Flagship department, the next step is to determine how you will achieve the additional sales.

Department sales records can tell you what sold in each junior department by class, style, color, and manufacturer. You scan computer sheet after computer sheet, looking for a clue that will lead to increased sales. An hour later, you realize you still don't have an answer to the question *how.*

Table 2.2   Opportunity Analysis by Merchandising Approach (Sales in 000s)

	Actual Sales	Potential Sales	Unrealized Opportunity
Flagship	$3,620	$4,433	$813
Branch #1	2,931	3,516	585
Branch #2	1,705	2,557	852
Branch #3	2,994	2,994	——

Table 2.3   Junior Sales/Junior % of Traffic

	Junior % of R-T-W Sales	*Junior % of All Customers*
Flagship	24.5%	45%
Branch #1	25	30
Branch #2	20	40
Branch #3	30	30

Looking through the files, you notice a folder marked "MARKETING INFORMATION." You pull the folder and resume your search for answers.

The information in Table 2.3 is the result of simple surveys and traffic counts in each of the store's units. It shows the percentage of junior customers that constitute the traffic in each unit. Your enthusiasm begins to return; this is the first piece of information about the consumer you have found.

You notice that the percentage of junior shoppers is the highest in the Flagship store and in Branch #2. However, those two units have the lowest junior-to-total sales relationship. Branch #3 seems right on target. In that unit, 30% of the customers that shop in the store are junior customers, and 30% of the total ready-to-wear business is done by the junior department. In contrast, junior customers total 45% of the Flagship traffic, yet that junior department contributes only 24.5% of the total ready-to-wear business.

You reason that if 45% of the customers who walk into the Flagship store are junior customers, there should be an opportunity for the junior area of that unit to contribute 45% of the total ready-to-wear business.

Now, instead of multiplying each unit's total ready-to-wear sales by 30%, the arbitrary standard you reached through the merchandising approach, you multiply the total sales figure by the percentage of junior customers who frequent each unit to come up with a potential sales amount. Then, as was done in Table 2.2, the actual sales are subtracted from the potential sales to arrive at the unrealized opportunity for the junior department in each unit. The unrealized opportunities results of the merchandising approach and the marketing approach are compared in Table 2.4.

Table 2.4   Unrealized Opportunities Comparison (Sales in 000s)

	Merchandising Approach	*Marketing Approach*
Flagship	$ 813	$3,029
Branch #1	585	585
Branch #2	852	1,705
Branch #3	——	——
	$2,250	$5,319

The marketing approach more than doubles the unrealized sales opportunity for the entire department. And, while the merchandising approach calculations indicated that both the Flagship store and Branch #2 had nearly equal sales/growth potential, $813,000 and $852,000 respectively, the marketing approach paints a very different picture. With the marketing approach, the Flagship has an unrealized opportunity of $3,029,000 compared to $1,705,000 for Branch #2.

But why, if the Flagship store is frequented by so many junior customers, are the junior department sales so low? You dig deeper into the "MARKETING INFORMATION" folder for more answers.

This pretend "MARKETING INFORMATION" folder has a wealth of information that can help you determine who the customer is and aid you in reaching your goal of increased sales. Where this information can be obtained will be covered in the next section. In reality, marketing information, while readily available, would not be sitting in a forgotten file.

Location profiles for Anyplace Department Stores reveal not only what surrounds each store, but provide clues about the customers who shop there and when the store gets its heaviest traffic. For instance, the Flagship store is in a business district of the city; office buildings, restaurants, and other retailers surround the Flagship store. There is a surge of customer traffic at lunch time and after office hours. Branch #2 is in an upscale mall in a residential section outside the city. The area's population is annually swelled by the students who attend the college located in the area.

Other information, obtained from credit card applications and credit card purchase records, gives you a clearer picture of the junior ready-to-wear customer in terms of age, marital status, and annual income. This *customer profile* information indicates that the junior customer is quite different at each unit. You also glean an important piece of information for the marketing puzzle from a shopping frequency study, as in Table 2.5.

A pure merchandising approach, with its focus on internal conditions and resource considerations, would call for similar merchandise mixes in all units. However, armed with the demographic information contained in the "MARKETING INFORMATION" folder, merchandise printouts of what sold in each unit, and your buyer's intuitive sense, you begin to picture the typical customer who walks into the junior department at each store. For example,

Table 2.5   Shopping Frequency—Junior Customers

	Shop Once a Week or More Often (%)
Flagship	35
Branch #1	20
Branch #2	16
Branch #3	17

Flagship—A young, single, working woman; entry-level or middle management position in the white-collar work force; comes into the department often, spends less on each purchase. Shopper groups: most are Young Contemporary, with some Moderate and Update.

Branch #2—A mixture of year-round customers (residents) and transient student customers (college); fashion needs are casual, but "special occasion" clothes are required in mix; cost is a consideration, but fashion tastes run in Classic, Update, and Trendy categories.

Now you have a better idea of the answer to the question of *who* purchases junior ready-to-wear at Anyplace Department Stores and are much closer to answering the question of *how* you will achieve the new sales goals at each unit.

Since the junior customers who shop the Flagship unit are in the store more often, you reason that the assortment there must continually look fresh and new. Displays and forward stock must be changed more often in that unit to capture the shoppers' interest and increase sales. In addition, you recognize that the assortment at the Flagship store must be primarily geared to a young working woman who lives alone, spends less per purchase, and wants an up-to-the-minute fashion look.

While that strategy is logical for increasing sales at the Flagship store, it would not be effective in Branch #2. To target the customers of this branch, you not only must know what will appeal to customers who are year-round residents, but have a finger on the pulse of the college customers' fashion needs.

The outward look afforded by marketing information gives the retailer important clues. Of course, the process was simplified for the purpose of illustration; however, marketing information helps the retailer take much of the guesswork out of such decisions as: What are the best price points, merchandise assortment, and merchandise presentation to reach the target customer?

Marketing data helps define one of the variables in the formula for retailing success: the customer. A retail store provides the framework for transactions to take place. Internal records indicate what the transaction was and when it took place, but offer no clues as to why it took place. By providing the dimension of consumer measurement, marketing information helps the retailer understand the forces that produced the results. It enables the retailer to understand and predict what it is that the customer wants.

Where to Get the Information

As we said earlier, some major retail operations employ a marketing person who, with the aid of a staff, could generate a folder of marketing information like the one "found" in the preceding example. In reality, marketing information is not as accessible or neatly arranged as it was in the Anyplace Department Stores scenario. However, marketing data is available to all retailers, big or small.

Marketing information comes from two sources: *primary data* and *secondary data*. Secondary data is information that is culled for the organization's purposes from existing studies or from existing information sources. Primary data is generated by the organization, and is geared to its specific circumstance and use.

We said the information contained in Table 2.3 was the result of simple surveys and *traffic counts*. This is an example of primary data. To generate that information, the marketing director deployed his staff at all the store's units to physically count the customers as they entered the store. Perhaps the traffic counters had a few questions to ask the customer: How often do you come into the store (frequency)? Are you a junior or missy customer? And so on. Perhaps the project was conducted for a period of time to arrive at averages and to allow for unusual traffic patterns, such as might be created with a special sale or a gift-giving holiday such as Valentine's Day.

Primary marketing data is complied in three ways: survey, observation, and experimentation. Surveys can be conducted through the mail, over the telephone, or with store interviews. Through the use of computers, the process could be totally automated, with the respondent keying in the answers to the questions that appear on the screen. Another way to "survey" the store customers is through the use of focus groups. A *focus group*, comprised of the store's customers—or a segment of the customer base, such as junior customers, male customers, people over 60 years of age—gives the retailer an opportunity to have direct contact and feedback with the very consumer the retailer is trying to reach. Focus group participants are invited in, usually with some sort of incentive, and asked questions about the store's services, advertising, merchandise offerings, etc.

Observation is the age-old method employed by retailers to determine who the customer is. In the case of the Flagship unit of Anyplace Department Stores, observation could yield important information about the junior customer. The fact that the women from the surrounding offices pour into the store between the hours of 12:00 noon and 2:00 P.M., and again after 5:00 P.M., dictates when additional sales personnel are needed and when special events should be scheduled. By noting what these women wear to work each day, it is possible to predict future needs and thus future sales.

Experimentation also yields important information. Let's say you requested the displays to be changed twice as often at the Flagship department and instructed your staff to change the forward stock more often. Your theory is that giving the department the look of newness and excitement will increase impulse sales. After a given period of time, evaluation of the sales results would prove or disprove the theory.

Secondary marketing data is information already available, albeit in another form. Company records can be a source of some information. If, for instance, a substantial amount of a store's sales are charges, information culled from the charge-customer files can be useful. Pertinent information can be obtained from the U.S. Census report, trade and consumer publications, buying offices, private research firms, and studies conducted by universities.

Within the trading area, the chamber of commerce, local banks, libraries, and local newspapers possess data that is useful to retailers. Often, the business departments at local colleges or universities will work with a retailer in conducting studies. Mall associations or local retailer groups often undertake studies, thus spreading the cost among their members.

The nuances of the trading area are obtained from less formalized sources of information. The radio talk show, the op-ed page of the local newspaper, what people are talking about, all lend useful insights to the retailer whose ear is tuned in. Information from all these sources, piece by piece, stratum by stratum, combine to give the retailer a clearer picture of the consumers he or she wishes to serve—and sell.

Summary

Marketing, and the information it provides, has become increasingly important to retail decision making. The marketing function looks outside the retail operation to understand the climate in which a retailer operates. It weaves demographic and psychographic information into the merchandising, sales promotion, and selling efforts of the retailer.

Marketing information comes from two sources, primary data and secondary data, and is available to all retailers regardless of size.

Since a retailer cannot measure each and every consumer in its trading area, groups are measured to understand and predict what goods and services can be profitably marketed to them. As with all grouping efforts, shopper segmentation reflects the average.

Terms for Review

1. Marketing concept
2. Demographics
3. Psychographics
4. Merchandising approach
5. Customer profile
6. Primary data
7. Secondary data
8. Traffic count
9. Focus group

Study Review Questions

1. Why does the need for marketing information increase as the distance between decision makers and the store's customers widens?
2. In what way does increased competition affect the need for marketing information?

3. What type of consumer measurements are supplied through marketing information?

4. What role does shopper segmentation play in retail decision making?

5. What is the difference between the pure merchandising approach and the marketing concept?

6. What marketing information can be generated by observation?

7. How would the retailer gain psychographic information about the target customer from the daily newspaper?

8. What role does the location of the store play?

Case

Your spouse has received an opportunity for a significant promotion and salary raise. It would, however, require relocation. After discussing the pros and cons of the move, you both decide to accept the offer.

You are employed in a large retail store. While you have spent your career with large retailers, you have always dreamed of having a small store of your own. You resign your position with the idea that the time is right to test your skills as an owner-operator.

You settle in a small college town within commuting distance of your spouse's new office. The atmosphere is quaint; most of the shops bordering the old town common have refurbished, old-fashioned facades. A small private college is located at one end of the town common; a large state university is within walking distance in the newer part of town.

You learn that one of the shops is for sale. The owner, an elderly gentleman, wants to retire and has no family. His operation, women's clothes and sportswear, is moderately successful. You have no problems with financing, his price is fair, and you decide to buy the store.

Questions

1. Where would you go to find demographic information? Psychographic information?

2. What could you learn from the other shopkeepers in the town? What information could the college and university supply? What insights would the old charge records offer?

3. How would this information help you decide what merchandise you should offer?

RETAIL SALES PROMOTION

The Sales Promotion Function

When we refer to *retail sales promotion,* we are speaking of all promotional efforts of a retail operation. Retail sales promotion involves communication activities that attract customers to the store and result in profitable sales. Another element of sales promotion is to build goodwill for the store, to ensure repeat business, and to establish a *customer base.*

A store is regularly engaged in several levels of communication with consumers. Personal selling is direct, one-to-one communication occurring between the store's sales force and the customer. The other components of sales promotion—advertising, visual merchandising or display, publicity, and special events—are, for the most part, indirect in nature.

Personal selling is an important aspect of sales promotion for the retailer. The salesperson is, after all, the last link in the chain of communication between the retailer and the customer, and very often the deciding factor in a sale. The last chapter of this book will deal with personal selling and the importance of that form of sales promotion. But for now, we will concentrate on the nonpersonal appeals that encourage business at the retail level.

The primary function of sales promotion is to stimulate customers to seek the merchandise or service promoted. The name of the game, and the road to a profitable business, is selling. But, to examine sales promotion as it is conducted today by the retailing industry, we must consider broader definitions and functions. The purpose of retail sales promotion is more than immediate sales gain.

A retailer's sales promotion effort consists of ideas that are developed, designed, and coordinated to communicate with the store's target audience. Sales promotion makes that audience aware of the store's existence, it creates an image of the store, it draws customers in, and it prompts purchasing. When executed efficiently, sales promotion is a blend of elements that combine to move the customer and retailer toward the desired interaction: sales.

The retailing industry is dynamic and responsive. It constantly changes, evolves, and adapts to a wide range of social and economic factors. The same is true of sales promotion. Today's news-making promotional tactic often is tired and ineffective tomorrow. The ideas for effective sales promotion must change and evolve to keep pace with the industry and to be responsive to the audience at which it is aimed. Yet certain principles for effective and cost-efficient sales promotion remain constant.

Throughout this book, we will be identifying those principles and giving you examples to illustrate them. Keep in mind, however, that while these principles can be applied to all sales promotion efforts, the situation particular to an individual store will determine its sales promotion needs and affect the execution of the sales promotion effort.

A prerequisite for an effective sales promotion program is determining *what* is to be accomplished, *why*, and *how* it is to be done. As elementary as this sounds, these basic determinations are often overlooked. The answers to these questions form the foundation on which all sales promotion activities are built.

In answering the questions of what, why, and how, there are four factors a retailer must consider:

- Desired image
- Reach and cost
- Coordination
- Creativity

DESIRED IMAGE

As a student of fashion and retailing, or as the owner-operator of a retail store, you already realize that determining store image is important to all retail operations planning.

The matter of store image influences what merchandise a store carries, what *price points* it offers, where the store is located, and even its physical design. Store image drives the services the store offers, its visual merchandising efforts, its hours of operation, the amenities such as dressing rooms, the method of payment, and so on—in short, all factors about the retail operation are determined by the image it wishes to project, and conversely, all of these image factors are determined by the customer it wishes to target.

Store image changes with its customers' wants and demands. For instance, when discount stores became a major retailing trend in the early 1980s, management found that the physical appearance of the stores and customer-comfort issues—for example, fixturing, lighting, and dressing rooms—were not important factors. Customers expected fewer frills from a discount store; they flocked to the discounter for the savings offered, and the discounter, in turn, saved on the image components "expected" of the regular-priced retailer. But as the market matured, and more discounters opened their doors, customers began to expect more. That is, in order to compete, the discounter had to add the very services and amenities that it had been able to previously eliminate.

Before any other decision about sales promotion can be made, a store's personality and image must be chosen. In deciding the store's image, management must take the target audience into account. In actuality, then, this first decision is based on a two-pronged question: whom do we wish to attract to the retail operation, and what personality do we wish to project to attract this audience?

Once the target audience has been defined, their needs and basic shopping and fashion viewpoints must be examined. As we discussed in Chapter 2, shopper segmentation translates social attitudes and behavior into corresponding shopping attitudes and purchasing behavior. Retailers use the characteristics ascribed to a shopper group to determine the shape and design of the sales promotion program.

For instance, is the shopper group(s) the store has decided will be targeted interested in price information? To what extent do they require facts about the product, its use, care, and warranty? Are they attracted by special sales, or are they more concerned with the store services?

You'll remember that Classic shoppers make planned, investment purchases and are responsive to store services. The shopping and purchasing behavior exhibited by the group provides a framework for the retailer's sales promotion program. Dollars spent promoting inexpensive or sale merchandise would be wasted on the Classic shopper. Instead, the store seeking to attract this shopper group should spend more promotional dollars at the start of a season, dwelling on store services and the investment benefits of the merchandise offered.

REACH AND COST

Once management has determined what store image and personality are to be projected, the communication vehicles to project that image must be examined. The question now becomes what vehicle will *reach* the target audience and what is the *relative cost*. In print advertising, for instance, the choices include but are not limited to daily newspapers, special newspaper inserts, direct mail, out-of-home advertising, and magazine advertising. We will look more closely at each of these vehicles in subsequent chapters; the point here is to understand that the elements of reach and cost are factors to consider when the retailer is choosing the vehicle best suited to deliver a message to its target customer. While one medium may be less expensive, the portion of the target audience reached through it may be substantially smaller than can be reached through another, more expensive vehicle.

Cost per thousand or *CPM* is a measurement commonly used to evaluate the reach/cost of an advertising vehicle. It is the cost of the ad divided by the vehicle's audience (readers, listeners, viewers). Representatives from both print and broadcast media have audience profiles and CPM information available. What complicates the reach/cost variable is the target audience factor.

Consider, as a simplified illustration, the decision facing the owner of an upscale bridal boutique. The owner knows from marketing information and experience that the Sunday edition of the local daily newspaper reaches the boutique's target customer, and that is where this retailer has historically spent a limited advertising budget. A representative from the newspaper contacts the owner with a new opportunity. The newspaper has decided to publish a special insert two times a year dedicated to weddings. "Weddings Today" will have feature articles on all aspects of planning a wedding and related topics such as choosing the ring, planning the honeymoon, and so on. The cost of an ad in this insert will be double the cost of running the same ad in the Sunday edition.

While the circulation for the insert is the same as the Sunday edition, and the cost of an ad in the insert is twice that for an ad in the Sunday edition, "Weddings Today" is actually a better advertising buy for bridal boutique owner. The reach/cost is affected by the fact that the insert will likely be saved, referred to, and reread by the very customer the bridal boutique is targeting.

COORDINATION

To achieve maximum effectiveness, elements of the sales promotion program must consist of a *unified blend*. That is to say, the various forms of sales promotion or communication with the target audience must complement and support one another. Without coordination, a weak, diffused communication takes place.

Coordination can be achieved both between the different elements of the sales promotion function and within the retail organization. The mutual support of the sales promotion elements increases the effectiveness and cost efficiency of any one. For example, a store's fall fashion story, conveyed to the target audience through a coordinated program of print ads, broadcast ads, window display, interior display, and special events, achieves a cumulative impact far greater than if each sales promotion vehicle were to carry a different message or theme.

Additionally, coordination between the different areas of the retail organization is required to achieve maximum results. A window display could effectively draw customers into the store, but if the salesperson is unaware of that display, the desired end result, sales, is impaired.

CREATIVITY

The factor of creativity is required in all aspects of successful retailing, but it is extremely significant to sales promotion. As consumers, we are bombarded daily with sales promotion messages. It is estimated that Americans are bombarded with over 3,000 advertising messages each day. Each seeks our attention and ultimately our action. Dull, unimaginative, unchanging promotions have little chance of capturing the attention of the target customer, especially when the clutter of advertising and sales promotion messages is considered.

The ability and skill to produce promotions with imagination and newness is a crucial, required factor in successful sales promotion. Even though the majority of sales promotion efforts are nondirect in nature, they cannot appear so if they are to reach the target customer. To be effective, to reach their mark, to deliver the intended communication, the sales promotion effort must appear to be a one-on-one, direct message to the target customer.

Taking these factors into account as they apply to the retailer's individual circumstances enable the retailer to determine what the sales promotion program should accomplish, why it is needed, and how it is to be conducted. To be successful, sales promotion must be part of a total marketing effort and consist of clear, planned objectives that are executed in a cost-efficient, coordinated, and creative way.

The Chain of Command

Now we will examine where the sales promotion function fits into the retail organization. As we have said, to be effective, sales promotion must be part of an overall marketing effort. It must be included as an important and equal aspect of the entire business.

The principal way to organize a retail operation is by function. Figure 3.1 shows the relationship of five retailing functions: merchandising, sales promotion, store operations, personnel, and control. Marketing is shown as a emerging function. It is growing out of the sales promotion function, since that area has historically carried out marketing activities. As a retailer becomes more committed to the marketing function, a new division for research and marketing emerges. It will influence decisions reached by the other five functions in the retail operation.

Figure 3.1

Emerging role and influence of the marketing function.

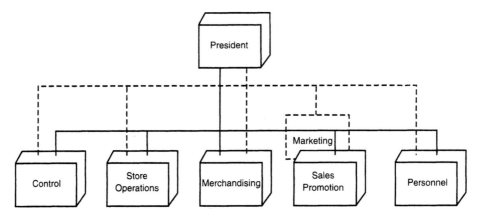

Where the sales promotion function is located in relation to the other retail functions is more important than who is actually performing the task. Figure 3.2 shows a segment of a typical *organizational chart* for a large retailer. In the case of an owner-manager retail operation, however, the president might perform the sales promotion activity in addition to other activities. Or the sales promotion function could be conducted by an outside consultant or firm.

How the organizational chart is broken down depends on the size of the retailer and the sales promotion needs of the retailer. As a general rule, the larger the organization, the more people needed to accomplish the task, and the more complicated the organizational chart.

Figure 3.2 represents a segment of a retailer's organizational chart. The sales promotion director and the general merchandise manager (a member of the merchandising division) both report directly to the president of the firm. Under each, the chain of command is broken down into lines of communication and responsibility. For instance, the window-display department reports to the visual merchandising or display director, who reports to the sales promotion director, who reports to the president. Fashion coordination, which works closely with both the merchandising and sales promotion functions, is below and between the two areas.

The sales promotion function, then, is broken down into areas of responsibility determined by store need. In a small store the sales promotion director may handle all elements of sales promotion alone or with a small staff. In larger stores the division of labor is such that the sales promotion director, often a vice president, is free for policy making and long-range planning. In a larger sense, the selling of goods is shared, in varying degrees, by both merchandising and sales promotion functions.

The Sales Promotion Budget

Now that we have the people in place, let's examine how the budget for sales promotion is decided.

The amount of money that a company spends on all its sales promotion activities is called the *sales promotion appropriation*. The sales promotion appropriation is a fixed percentage of the *anticipated annual sales*. Management uses anticipated rather that last year's sales figures because there is an accepted correlation between the amount of sales promotion conducted and the resulting sales. Therefore, the sales promotion budget is determined by the amount of sales the firm wants to achieve.

The *fixed percentage* applied to the *net sales* can be as low as 1.5% or as high as 6%. Generally, the total promotional expense of most stores does not exceed 4–5% of the total net sales.

Once the overall budget has been decided, the appropriation is then allocated to the various sales promotion activities.

There are several methods used by retailers to reach the overall sales promotion budget. You will note that each has advantages and disadvantages.

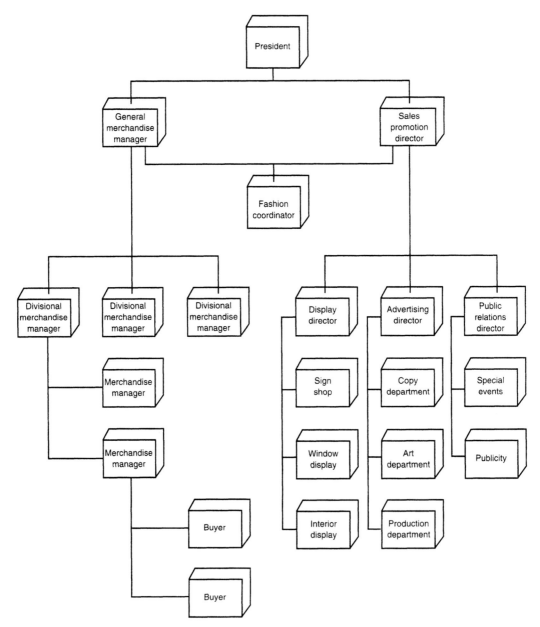

Figure 3.2
Example of a retailer's organizational chart.

TOP-TO-BOTTOM METHOD

Just as it sounds, this method of determining a sales promotion budget originates with top management.

Management designates goals for sales volume over six-month and total-year periods. Then, these sales goals are multiplied by the predetermined appropriation percentage to arrive at a total sales promotion budget. This total amount is then allocated to the various sales promotion activities and subdivided into specific forms of sales promotion. In Figure 3.3, the allocation for advertising has been further divided into budgets for the various forms of advertising media. Next, shares of these funds are allocated to the store's merchandise divisions, and then to departments. This step would then be repeated with all areas of sales promotion.

This method is most widely used by large, well-established retailers whose sales volume has reflected steady growth throughout the years. The top-to-bottom method allows top management tight control of promotion expenses in relation to the store's total sales volume.

The disadvantage of this method is that it does not utilize the insights that merchandise managers and their buyers possess. Their direct exposure to market information and the customer often provides valuable information regarding promotional opportunities to increase volume.

BOTTOM-TO-TOP METHOD

This method gives the merchandising division, or the departments within a specific division, the task of planning the sales promotion appropriation. The theory behind this method is that the buyers and merchandise managers are closer to the customer and to merchandise acceptance and thus are in a better position to estimate sales goals.

The budget is established by merchandise division or by department. Estimates of sales promotion needs are made on a day-to-day, week-to-week basis. For example, the merchandise manager and buyer estimate how many lines of advertising their area will need to reach the sales goal in a particular week. The resulting figures are combined for the advertising budget for a six-month and then a yearly period.

The disadvantage of this method is that top management loses control of the sales promotion expenditures. Also, since each area is working independently, the store's overall sales promotion mix and message is sacrificed.

ALL-ONE-CAN-AFFORD METHOD

While this method is not widely used, and is less effective than a well-thought-out, planned program, a store may resort to this method when the business climate has altered suddenly.

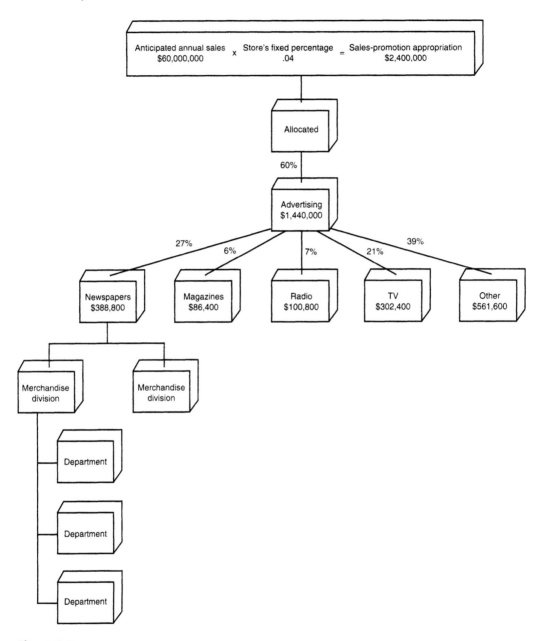

Figure 3.3
Advertising segment of top-to-bottom budgeting method.

The most likely reason to use this method is to meet the sales promotion expenditures of a store's competition. New, aggressive competition may force a retailer into a defensive position.

The other two methods rely on consistent buying and purchasing habits. However, unpredictability is a growing factor in our uncertain economy. Conditions such as fluctuating consumer demand and sales volume, changing practices of resources, and the need to reevaluate sales estimates periodically make this method an attractive alternative for some retailers.

THE COMBINATION OF METHODS

Ideally, a retailer should use a combination of all three methods in planning the sales promotion appropriation. Management should get input from those closest to the customer to get a better idea of the sales promotion needs of individual areas. Reserve money, as much as 20% of the total sales promotion budget, is commonly set aside to allow for the unexpected crisis or opportunity. By controlling the sales promotion appropriation and overall policy, management ensures that the sales promotion message is consistent and strong.

Once the sales promotion appropriation is determined, regardless of the method, it is allocated to the various elements of sales promotion. These allocations are further divided among the forms of a specific element. In Figure 3.3, this has been done for advertising. The total amount budgeted for advertising has been broken down into media categories: newspaper, magazines, radio, TV, and other. The next step is to break down the total store newspaper budget into newspaper budgets for each merchandise division and finally for each department.

The percentage of the sales promotion appropriation allocated to a division or department varies. The figure is based on the merchandise involved and the demands of local competition. Generally, the percentage allotted is higher for fashion departments than for semistaple or staple goods departments. This percentage is based upon experience (what the store has done in the past) and national averages (what others are doing). The percentage can also change, sometimes dramatically.

Consider, for a moment, bed linens. A lot has changed in that category since your grandmother's biggest concern was how to keep them white. Add some color, a pattern, and a designer name, and what was once a staple item becomes a fashion item and a *growth area*. That is, bed linens become a merchandise classification that has the opportunity for increased sales volume. It now does more than cover the bed and the occupant—it is a fashion choice, based on taste, style, and personal self-image. There is increased competition; there is an increased need for communication. The sales promotion allocation for that category therefore increases.

There is another factor to consider when allocating the sales promotion appropriation. Remember that the first two methods, top-to-bottom and bottom-to-top, based their calculations on sales goals. The goals vary from month to month. Sales patterns tend to repeat themselves year after year. Despite outside influences—wars, inflation, population shifts—the overall sales pattern remains fairly consistent. February, for example, is a slow month for retailers; December is the busiest. The retailer allots the budget monthly according to the percentage of the total years' business historically done in a particular month.

INCLUDED IN THE BUDGET

What is charged against the sales promotion appropriation? One obvious answer is the media costs: the cost of a newspaper ad, a TV commercial, a billboard rental. But other, less obvious costs are planned for in the sales promotion appropriation, for example,

- The sales promotion payroll, including on-staff personnel, freelance people hired for special jobs, and consultants called in for advisory services
- Cost of supplies, including cuts, mats, display materials, paper, art supplies, sign cards, ink, paints, and so on
- Postage and distribution charges for publicity and mailing lists
- Travel charges for the staff to travel to professional meetings, shows, and exhibits
- Miscellaneous, unforeseen factors, including lost display merchandise

The actual size of the sales promotion appropriation varies from store to store and is dependent on many factors. It is influenced by how old or new a store is, how famous or unknown. It is dependent on the size of the store, its location, the size of the trading area, the kinds of merchandise carried, the amount and type of competition, and the amount and type of advertising the competition conducts. It is dependent on the cost of the available media, the traffic the store already enjoys, and business conditions in general.

Planning—The Sales Promotion Calendar

The *sales promotion calendar* is the store's master plan for sales promotion. It is a combination of historical fact and future plans. It lists the sales achieved last year, the planned sales for the current year, and the sales promotion efforts that will help bring about those sales. It lists the amount of money spent on sales promotion last year, providing a basis for comparison.

The sales promotion calendar is vital for achieving coordination and control over the sales promotion program. It ensures that the correct amount of money is spent within a given period of time to reach the desired sales volume. It charts the activities that will be conducted, the expense of those activities, and where the responsibility for conducting those activities lies.

Some events or promotional opportunities are determined by external forces. National holidays, planned events in the locale, or a promotion sponsored by the merchant's association or mall association are examples of externally prompted events. Promotional campaigns run by the competition or events sponsored by a manufacturer or trade association will also determine some of the store's promotions.

Other events are internal in nature. Anniversary sales, month-end sales, and institutional campaigns are determined by store history and custom. Fashion and prestige promotions—instruments for establishing the desired store image—are also internally prompted.

Some promotions fall in between these two categories. The annual housewares sale retailers conduct in March probably can be attributed to internal tradition, competitors' sales, and outside support from manufacturers and/or trade associations.

There are necessary steps in creating a sales promotion calendar for any retail institution, regardless of its size. We will now go through each step and, in the process, create a sales promotion calendar for Simple Specialty Store as in Figures 3.4 and 3.5. Obviously, the larger the retailer, the more complex the sales promotion calendar, since different trading areas, target audiences, and available media have to be considered. The steps, however, are the same for the larger retailer.

Several items are indispensable when preparing the sales promotion calendar: a list of national holidays, a list of local events, and last year's calendar. With these tools assembled, we begin to enter the following:

1. *Historical information*—last year's actual sales figures and sales promotion expenses by month to provide a basis for comparison and guidance for the current year's plan. You'll notice that Figure 3.4 has the total store sales for last year at the top right and last year's sales broken down by each month. Last year's sales promotion expenses are handled in the same fashion.

2. *Planned sales goals*—the store's total six-month and yearly sales goals broken down by month using past sales patterns as a guide. Larger stores break the year into two halves, giving them more flexibility to adjust their projections according to market or economic influences. For our purposes, we will plan the total year's sales at $1,000,000. Since a condominium opened in town last month, attracting the type of customer we want to target, we feel confident we can achieve a healthy sales increase. To get the planned sales by month, we multiply $1,000,000 by the percentage of the total year's business normally done in that particular month. Historically, for instance, we have done 6.6% of the total year's business in the month of January—$1,000,000 × .066 = $66,000.

3. *Needed promotion*—the promotion the store requires to reach the sales goals. Factors influencing this decision include type of store, store location, types of competition, available media, and general business conditions. Evaluation

Sales Promotion Calendar for Simple Specialty Store		
Total Store Sales	$800,000	$1,000,000
Total sales-promotion expenses	$32,000	$40,000
Minus 10% reserve fund		$4,000
Total allocation:		$36,000
65% -- Advertising	$23,400	
20% -- Public relations	$7,200	
15% -- Display	$5,400	

January		February		March		April		May		June	
Sales:		**Sales:**		**Sales:**		**Sales:**		**Sales:**		**Sales:**	
Last year	Planned	Last year	Planned	Last year	Planned	Last year	Planned	Last year	Planned	Last year	Planned
$52,800	$66,000	$50,400	$63,000	$60,000	$75,000	$65,600	$82,000	$60,800	$76,000	$60,000	$75,000
Sales promotion expenses:		**Sales promotion expenses:**		**Sales promotion expenses:**		**Sales promotion expenses:**		**Sales promotion expenses:**		**Sales promotion expenses:**	
Last year	Planned	Last year	Planned	Last year	Planned	Last year	Planned	Last year	Planned	Last year	Planned
$2,112	$2,376	$2,016	$2,268	$2,400	$2,700	$2,624	$2,952	$2,432	$2,736	$2,400	$2,700
Early Bird Bathing Suit Sale and Free Vacation Contest		President's Birthday Sale				Annual Anniversary Sale				Special Event: Simple Specialty's Bike-a-Thon for Hospital Charity	

July		August		September		October		November		December	
Sales:		**Sales:**		**Sales:**		**Sales:**		**Sales:**		**Sales:**	
Last year	Planned	Last year	Planned	Last year	Planned	Last year	Planned	Last year	Planned	Last year	Planned
$59,200	$74,000	$65,600	$82,000	$64,000	$80,000	$68,800	$86,000	$75,200	$94,000	$117,600	$147,000
Sales promotion expenses:		**Sales promotion expenses:**		**Sales promotion expenses:**		**Sales promotion expenses:**		**Sales promotion expenses:**		**Sales promotion expenses:**	
Last year	Planned	Last year	Planned	Last year	Planned	Last year	Planned	Last year	Planned	Last year	Planned
$2,368	$2,664	$2,624	$2,952	$2,560	$2,880	$2,752	$3,096	$3,008	$3,384	$4,704	$5,292
Founding Father's Dollar Day Sale		Fall Fashion Show Brierwood Country Club				Distance for Dimes Marathon		Election Day Sales		Men's only Hot Toddy Christmas Shopping Party	

Figure 3.4

of the store's own experience and the experience of others serve as a guide. Often stores use a fixed percentage (generally 4–5%) of net sales to reach the sales promotion appropriation. Since 4% has always worked in the past for Simple Specialty, we will again use it to reach a sales appropriation of $40,000.

4. *Reserve budget*—a cushion to avoid overspending and cover the unforeseen crisis or opportunity. Many stores reserve 10%, some as high as 20%.

5. *Allocation*—the sales promotion appropriation divided among the various sales promotion activities. This step is also influenced by available media, cost of media, past experience, and competition. Other expenses classifications, such as salaries and supplies, are budgeted in each area at this point.

			Simple Specialty Store			
Sales Promotion Calendar Month: December			Total planned sales promotion expenses: *$5.292* Advertising: *$3.440* Public Relations: *$1.058* Display: *$794*			
Sunday	Monday	Tuesday	Wednesday	Thursday	Friday	Saturday
		1	2	3	4 *AD* *Christmas* *Windows*	5
6	7 *Town's* *tree lighting* *ceremony* *store open* *'til 10 pm*	8	9 *Send out* *Hot Toddy* *Party* *invitations*	10	11 *AD*	12
13 *Men's only* *Hot Toddy* *Party* *AD*	14	15	16 *AD* *(include* *Hot Toddy* *Party* *reminder)*	17	18 *Men's only* *Hot Toddy* *Christmas* *Shopping Party* *6-9 pm*	19
20 *Institutional* *Christmas* *ad*	21	22 *Stocking-* *Stuffer* *Gifts* *AD*	23	24 *Store closes* *4 pm*	25 *Christmas* *Day*	26
27	28	29	30	31		

Figure 3.5

Since there haven't been major changes in available media or our competition from last year, 65% of the sales promotion appropriation will go to advertising, 20% to public relations, and the remaining 15% to display.

6. *Store monthly budget*—the classification budget broken down into monthly budgets. Promotion expenditures should parallel the monthly sales curve determined in step 2. For example, December historically has contributed 14.7% of the store's total business. We multiply the store's total sales promotion appropriation by 14.7% to arrive at December's appropriation—$5,292. This is done for each of the 12 months.

Now that the monthly total sales promotion expenses have been determined, a master plan by month is created. Using the percentages determined in step 5, the total monthly figure is allocated to each of the sales promotion activities: advertising, public relations, and display. Figure 3.5 illustrates this process for the month of December. You will also note in Figure 3.5 that we already can sketch out some of the "events" and pinpoint some of the activities, even this far in advance. We know, for instance, that the town's big tree lighting event will occur on December 7 and that the store will stay open late. We also slot the stocking stuffer gift ad to run on December 22, based on past success with this ad on this date. At this point in time, we have not determined what will run in the ad, or even the total cost of the ad. We are still at the broad-brush stroke phase of planning.

The next step is to take the sales promotion calendar and fine-tune it further. *Department budgets* or what each division or department is allocated within the monthly sales promotion budget is the next step. As we discussed earlier, the percentage of the sales promotion appropriation varies from department to department, and from month to month. Other factors, added to our past experience, must be considered. Ladies' gloves, for example, would traditionally be advertised during the cold weather months. But input from the fashion coordinator, who predicts the glove in all price points to be a major fashion item in spring, would necessitate an adjustment to that department's traditional allocation. *Major promotions* the retailer plans for the upcoming year, such as storewide events, department events, annual events, institutional campaigns, special events, and prestige promotions, are entered onto the Master Sales Promotion Calendar and are considered when determining the allocation each department receives of the total sales promotion budget.

The *monthly sales promotion plan*—the detailed plan created six to eight weeks prior to a given month—is when the creativity and the "finger-on-the-pulse" excitement of retailing comes into play. By this time we know our customer (from marketing information), we know what we have to offer that meets a need, we know what vehicle will best reach the target customer, and we are ready to communicate. The specifics of advertising, that is, the size of the ad, the vehicle, the dates, the prices, and so on, are listed. Simultaneously, support sales promotion elements are scheduled: direct mail, window display, special events.

The final plan—*the daily advertising plan*—includes the day-to-day roughs made from the master plan calendar with the necessary adjustments.

Summary

All companies engage in some form of sales promotion. Unless a firm can communicate the existence of the product produced or the service offered, no sales can take place. Retail sales promotion involves communication between the store and its target customer.

Personal salesmanship is the direct form of sales promotion; advertising, visual merchandising, and publicity are indirect forms. However, the more database marketing is employed, the more "direct" these aspects of sales promotion become.

Successful sales promotion is part of a total marketing effort, consisting of clear, planned objectives that are executed in a cost-efficient, coordinated, and creative way. To chart the sales promotion activities, keep track of the sales promotion expenses, and assign responsibility, retailers rely on the sales promotion calendar.

Terms for Review

1. Retail sales promotion
2. Customer base
3. Price points
4. Reach
5. CPM
6. Unified blend
7. Organizational chart
8. Sales promotion appropriation
9. Anticipated annual sales
10. Fixed percentage
11. Net sales
12. Growth area
13. Sales promotion calendar

Study Review Questions

1. How does personal selling differ from the retailer's other sales promotion communication?
2. What forms the foundation of all sales promotion activities?
3. How does the store's desired image affect sales promotion activities?
4. What does coordination mean in terms of a retailer's sales promotion campaign?
5. Why is creativity important in retail sales promotion?
6. What are the three methods of determining the sales promotion budget? Identify the advantages and disadvantages of each.
7. Why are sales promotion budget figures based on planned sales instead of last year's actual sales? Name some of the conditions that could change the retailer's marketing strategy.
8. Why do sales goals vary from month to month? Wouldn't it be easier to divide the store's total sales goal by 12?
9. What information does a sales promotion calendar reveal about a store?

Case

Someplace Specialty is located in the residential area of a medium-sized city. "Sleepy" is the term that best characterizes its business. Mr. Willowbee has owned and operated the small store for 20 years. As the neighborhood changed around him, tenements giving way to high-rise cooperatives and rental apartment buildings, Mr. Willowbee made very few changes in his sales promotion efforts. While he has tried to update his merchandise to reflect the tastes of the working women who have moved into the neighborhood, he feels that the audience he wishes to attract doesn't know he is open and ready to do business.

You meet Mr. Willowbee in the line at the bank. He starts talking about his concern: since the rent for his store has doubled this year, he needs to attract more customers if his business is going to survive. He knows that sales promotion is part of the answer, but he doesn't know how to go about changing his ads, how much he should budget, or even where to look for information on which to base his decisions.

He tells you that he has decided to hire a "sales promotion director" to handle the problem. This person would have to handle all aspects of sales promotion for the store.

Your job experience, in the advertising department of a larger retailer in the city, has given you a background in ad preparation. You feel that that credential, combined with your knowledge of retail sales promotion from your college courses, qualifies you for the job. Mr. Willowbee is not quite convinced, so you agree to prepare a sales promotion budget and calendar for the next six months. If Mr. Willowbee likes them, you have the job.

Questions

1. Before you begin, what information would you need to obtain from Mr. Willowbee?
2. What additional information would you seek and from where?
3. Why would a list of upcoming events in the city be important?

THE ADVERTISING DEPARTMENT

Advertising is an important aspect of sales promotion. It reaches out to the consumer and communicates with him or her. It creates awareness, carves the store's image, provides information about a new product or latest fashion, and prompts action. By its very definition, advertising is a powerful form of communication. Whether we like to admit it or not, advertising influences our attitudes, preferences, and behavior.

Effective retail advertising is the result of input from the store's management, from its merchants, and from its sales promotion experts. This chapter will deal with the function those experts perform and how they budget for it. And, we will begin to see what distinguishes retail advertising from conventional consumer advertising.

Role of the Agency

It has been estimated that only one-half of all money spent on advertising is spent through advertising agencies. The other half is spent directly by companies that prepare their own advertising. These companies include department stores, supermarkets, and small businesses. Why is that?

It is basically the way advertising agencies are structured that makes it difficult for them to serve retailers. Approximately four-fifths of the $15 billion annually spent on advertising through agencies is spent by full-service agencies. These agencies are staffed by teams of highly skilled technical and creative people who develop, prepare, and place advertising for clients in the various media. Additionally, the *full-service advertising agency* assists the client in every phase of marketing planning, sales promotion, merchandising, packaging, public relations, and market research. Advertising agencies have evolved into highly specialized marketing intermediaries who specialize in selling advertising and marketing skills. They are usually able to offer these services and perform these tasks for less than it would cost an individual firm to do so even if it were feasible for the individual firm to hire all these experts. That is, with the exception of most retailers.

The answer, in a word, is timing. Agencies are not geared to the "bat 'em out" approach to advertising that retailers by necessity must take. Retail advertising—especially newspaper and radio advertising—is seldom finalized more than one or two days before it runs. Last-minute determinations are basic to the nature of retailing and its advertising; agencies, due to their intensive specialization, are not geared to this.

It is also difficult for the agency to work with the many people who have input into retail advertising. The decisions about effective retail advertising are reached only after there is input from management and the merchandising and sales promotion divisions. The agency kitchen is not designed for so many cooks.

And there is the matter of cost. The full-service agency requires more time to prepare an ad, and the costs are higher than if the retailer works directly with the media (as do small stores) or maintains an advertising department.

Some advertising agencies have established special "retail advertising departments" that handle last-minute changes and quick deadlines. More commonly, however, the relationship between the advertising agency and the retailer is specialized.

Retailers may retain advertising agencies to undertake a major institutional or image-building campaign. Some retailers use an agency for radio and television advertising alone. An agency is sometimes called upon for special advertising material, special research, or counsel on planning and copy concepts.

For some large retailers, an advertising agency is the logical choice for obtaining the level of creativity and professionalism needed to accomplish a major task, such as a change in store image.

For example, Figure 4.1 is an example of an agency-produced ad that ran in major consumer magazines. Sears' goal is to establish the store as a fashion source—and to increase sales in its fashion departments. The campaign—"Come see the softer side of Sears"—builds upon the strong market position and image the retailer already enjoys—that of a resource for quality hardware, tools, automobile supplies—and then "marries" it to the image of a store that has a wide selection of fashion items at a reasonable price.

In this two-page print ad, a well-known Sears brand, the DieHard battery, is juxtaposed with a fashion shot. The comparison is jarring and, therefore, effective. What could be more opposite than a car battery and a black crepe cocktail dress? The companion ads are opposite not only in product, but in presentation. The DieHard ad is stark with its use of white space; the fashion shot is produced in warm hues. The clever copy is a play on words: "I came in for a DieHard. And left with something drop dead."

The ads work together to project Sears as a store that offers fashion at a reasonable price. The dress is designer quality—the price, $72.00, is in line with that retailer's target customer's budget. In addition to print advertising, the "Softer

Side of Sears" campaign utilizes other media, including television. This level of creativity and extensive use of the media is an example of when the retailer is best served by the talents of a full-service agency. It is doubtful that the store's own staff could have stepped back and made such creative use of the diverse products the store offers while targeting a fashion customer.

The Ad Men and Women

There is no correct organization for a retail advertising department. The individual titles and responsibilities are less important than the work the department achieves. In fact, the small retailer is forced to perform these functions solo, or with the help made available by the various media.

There are three major components that make up the retail advertising function: *copy, art,* and *production.* Copy is all written materials that appear in a print ad and the text or script that is used for a broadcast commercial. Art is the visual component of the advertisement. It encompasses the physical appearance of the ad, its design, and its presentation. Production is the component of the advertising function that is responsible for producing the final result.

COPY—THE SALES MONOLOGUE

Advertising copy is a one-way message designed to inspire action. *Copywriters,* the people who produce the copy, are salespeople who utilize their writing skill to sell. They are called upon to write the text for print ads and the scripts for television and radio commercials, and to create eye-catching headlines or slogans that will set the store apart from its competition.

It is important to remember that no matter what the theme of the advertisement, the primary job of the copywriter is to sell the store. The copy may be for a sale ad or for the store's holiday greeting, but the ultimate goal of a good copywriter is to sell the benefits of that particular retailer.

The copywriter must be able to translate product information and consumer research data into copy that will trigger the desired response. To be able to communicate persuasively, the copywriter must know what the target customer's needs and aspirations are and the image the store wants to project. Meaningful copy talks directly to that customer, sparking interest and inspiring action.

ART—PLANNING AND EXECUTING IDEAS

Another component of advertising—art—is less easily defined since it comprises many facets. There is usually one person who oversees this component of advertising. For our purposes, we will refer to this overseer and coordinator as the *art director,* but the title is not important.

"*I came in for a DieHard.*"

Figure 4.1

The jarring use of opposites, both in product and ad layout, make these companion ads effective in grabbing the reader's attention and communicating that Sears has another—softer—side. Courtesy of Sears, Roebuck and Co.

Figure 4.1 (continued)

The art director is responsible for the physical appearance of an advertisement, its design, and its effectiveness. This person is involved in the advertising process from the conception of the ad to the point at which it is turned over to production. Working with the copywriter, the art director helps develop the concept of the ad. Next, the art director chooses and then oversees the work of the illustrator or photographer who can best implement the concept of the ad, chooses the *type* that will be used, and decides the *layout* or design of the ad.

The art component is the coordination of all visual elements. This includes the selection of props, models, locations, even a say in the merchandise to be featured. The art director must also coordinate all the people needed to execute the store's advertising. In addition to staff members, the art director oversees everyone from graphic designers, artists, and photographers for print, to TV producers, actors, and musicians for broadcast. This responsibility demands skills in problem solving, the ability to think creatively, and the ability to work with and motivate people.

PRODUCTION—THE BLUEPRINT OF ADVERTISING

The final component of the advertising function is production. Production has the responsibility for the final result. Schedules must be established to control the flow and timing of the work so that deadlines can be met. This area works with outside services such as printers, engravers, and others needed for the mechanical production of the final advertising product. Production is the nuts-and-bolts function that turns the creative ideas of art and copy into reality.

The Advertising Ratio

As we discussed in Chapter 3, the percentage of the sales promotion appropriation allocated to the different areas of the store varies from department to department. This percentage is called the *advertising ratio.*

Determination of an advertising ratio depends on several factors. Past experience, local market conditions, size and type of the department, and the retailer's specific objectives all have to be taken into account. Retailers also look to their competition, drawing guidance from national averages and inspiration from a "success story." And, as we have already discussed, the ratio used in the past may be invalid if the merchandise classification is suddenly influenced by the forces of fashion and has been earmarked as a growth department.

A department's ad budget is reached by multiplying the advertising ratio by the six-month planned sales. Let's say that your department, women's hosiery and gloves, has a six-month planned sales goal of $15,000. Historically, your store has found that an advertising ratio of 2.5% is appropriate for the department and in keeping with the national average. By multiplying the planned sales by the advertising ratio, you find the department has an ad budget of $375.

However, last month one of your competitors, a hosiery specialty store, went out of business. Management has indicated that capturing that store's displaced customers should be one of your objectives. You and the merchandise manager decide that for this six-month period the advertising ratio should be increased to 3.0%. You now have an advertising budget of $450.

After the advertising ratio has been used to determine the advertising budget for the department, the budget is then broken down into a *monthly department advertising budget.*

Remember we said that retail business fluctuates by month. Each merchandise classification or department in a store has its heavy and light selling periods. The concept is logical if you stop and think about it: gloves would be in greater demand during the fall and winter months than during the scorching summer months.

The department's advertising budget should be spent or budgeted in accordance with this historical sales fluctuation. If business is historically slow during a particular month, advertising dollars spent during that time period would be wasted. The ad would not increase interest or prompt sales; fur-lined gloves just aren't on your customers' minds during the summer.

However, circumstances could change an historic monthly department advertising budget. Just as the advertising ratio was adjusted for a change in competition, and the opportunity to capture new customers, the monthly budget could veer from the norm if affected by a fashion trend.

For example, the new "fad" embraced by teenagers is the full length, above-the-elbow glove. It is so hot that the well-dressed would not be caught dead without these gloves at the prom or other formal affairs. While May and June were not traditional months to budget advertising for the glove and hosiery department, spending dollars to attract business this year makes complete sense.

The Advertising Plan

The *advertising plan* is really an advertising calendar like the sales promotion calendar. It is a forecast for a specified period of time (usually six months) of the advertising a store intends to utilize to attract customers. The word "forecast" is important. The advertising plan for a particular month is reworked and adjusted about a month in advance to answer the needs of the store and to allow for unforeseen changes. Last-minute changes are necessitated by everything from hot-seller items to problems in merchandise delivery.

The advertising plan includes the following data:

- Date of ad
- Department and item(s) to be advertised
- Estimated sales from ad
- Medium used for ad

- Amount of space (print) or time (broadcast)
- Cost of ad

In a large retail organization, the advertising plan consists of two parts, the *whole-firm plan* and the *divisional plan.*

The whole-firm plan is just as it sounds: it is the advertising plan that incorporates the objectives of the whole firm as well as the individual departments or divisions. The whole-firm advertising plan establishes the advertising allocation for the company for a specific period of time. It outlines the major objectives and the major selling events.

The whole-firm plan outlines the amount of advertising dollars budgeted for the various media. Each advertising medium budget is then allotted to individual departments or divisions. It identifies the selling events planned by the firm that each division or department is expected to participate in.

After the whole-firm plan has been determined, it is given to the divisions or departments to serve as a basis for their detailed divisional plan.

The divisional plan (or department plan, depending on the size of the store and its policies) gets down to specifics. It lists the types of merchandise to be featured, types of promotion to be conducted, price points and conditions of sale, the medium, and the timing of all these factors. It is conducted for a six-month time period and is then refined a month in advance of the actual selling month.

All the planning that we are discussing is not pulled from thin air. It is the result of past experience, present conditions, and future expectations. And it is based on solid data. Both the whole-firm and divisional plans make use of the following information:

- Advertising department records indicating how an ad was done, at what cost, and with what sales results
- Last year's and previous year's sales
- This year's sales goals
- Last year's special events and results
- Last year's special sales events and results
- List of this year's calendar changes and holidays compared with last year's
- List of major competitors' events last year
- List of major competitors' key items or line promotions last year
- List of important municipal, state, or national events that have tie-in potential
- List of special media events for tie-ins
- Marketing facts
- Vendor and industry events or programs

These records and data provide a basis from which realistic plans can be formulated. But for the retailer, "plans" are just that. To be successful, that is, to communicate effectively with the target customer and produce sales, the advertising the retailer conducts must be timed and constructed in such a way that it reaches that customer. The underlying message of the retail ad is "We have what you want, desire, and need, and we have it now."

Summary

Retail advertising is a unique form of consumer advertising. Its special needs prevent most retailers from utilizing an advertising agency for day-to-day ads, but an agency may be called in for special projects and/or for broadcast advertising.

Retail advertising can be broken down into the components of copy, art, and production.

A department or division is allotted a portion of the store's advertising ratio for the area. The budget is further broken down into monthly budgets, coinciding with the percentage of business expected to be done in a given month.

All the planning is based on past experience (as documented in numerous store records), present conditions (marketing data), and future expectations. The plan must have flexibility built into it, due to the changeable nature of retailing.

Terms for Review

1. Full-service agencies
2. Copy
3. Art
4. Production
5. Copywriter
6. Art director
7. Type
8. Layout
9. Advertising ratio
10. Monthly department advertising budget
11. Advertising plan
12. Whole-firm plan
13. Divisional plan

Study Review Questions

1. What does advertising accomplish for the retailer?
2. Explain the factors in the retailing industry that make a full-service advertising agency a poor choice for the day-to-day ads for the retailer.
3. When would a retailer employ an ad agency?
4. What are the components that make up the retail advertising function?
5. What is the ultimate goal of the copywriter? Why?
6. How is a store's or department's advertising ratio determined?
7. What are some conditions that would change an established advertising ratio?
8. What is the relationship between sales fluctuations and the advertising budget?

9. What three factors affect the advertising plan?
10. Why are last year's advertising efforts important in planning this year's forecast?

 ## Case

Specialty Store, Inc. caters to a Young Contemporary and Advanced customer. As physical fitness became increasingly popular, the owner started to add fashion exercise clothes and gear to the merchandise mix. So far, most of the department's sales have been impulse purchases: the customer has come into the store for something else and, seeing the exercise clothes, has purchased them.

The owner has just heard that a fully equipped health spa is opening next month two blocks away from the store.

Questions

1. Explain the significance, if any, of this development in the retailer's marketplace.
2. What effect would the spa have on Specialty Store, Inc.'s advertising ratios?
3. Why would it be a good idea for the owner of Specialty Store, Inc. to speak to the management of the new spa?

5 *TYPES OF RETAIL ADVERTISING*

Retail advertising is a nonpersonal form of communication. It is a message from a store to a current or prospective customer.

Retail advertising announces that a store has anticipated and is prepared to meet consumer needs. So while this form of sales promotion is categorized as nonpersonal, effective retail advertising is, in fact, personalized. To anticipate its customer's needs accurately, the store must "know" its customers; in order for customers to recognize that the communication was meant for them, the message must be a personal, targeted expression.

Retailers employ various types of ads to reach their customers. Each type of ad is designed to accomplish a different goal. The ad may be designed to produce large unit sales and profit for the store. Or, as with a *loss-leader ad*, where one item or several items are offered at a price which will produce little or no profit for the retailer, the intent is to build store traffic, to get customers into the store, and, it is hoped, to increase total store sales. The advertising may be designed to establish or reinforce the store's image, or its intent may be public service. No matter what the obvious intent of a particular ad, the ultimate goal of all retail advertising is to sell the store, the sponsor of the ad.

For an effective advertising effort, a store employs a mix of retail ads. A mix of ad types balances the communication and reaches more prospective customers. A message that will "reach" or perk one customer's interest may be ineffective for another customer. Just how many of each type a store employs depends on the image the store wishes to project and the kind of customers the retailer seeks to attract.

In this chapter, we will examine the advertising conducted by retailers by category. While the examples chosen to illustrate these categories are from newspapers, the categories also apply to retailers' advertising in other vehicles, such as broadcast or out-of-home.

Institutional Advertising

Retailers earmark a portion of the advertising budget to sell more than the current goods they are offering. These advertising dollars are spent to "sell" or attract their customers over a long period of time, to keep the customers returning to the store's door. *Institutional advertising* sells the establishment itself. The institutional ad builds upon or attempts to establish the reputation of the store—its character, its reliability—in the minds of the target audience.

Often the approach for an institutional ad is prestige. The message in this type of institutional ad is about the quality of the merchandise carried, the brands or designer names available, the depth of merchandise selection, or the exclusivity of the store's offerings. Store services or store facilities are also common themes of *prestige ads* if these elements set the store apart from its competition.

Another type of institutional advertising is the *policy ad*. Policy ads convey to the customer what the store stands for. The character of the store is communicated through messages about store services, store hours, conditions of sale (credit cards, layaway plan, etc.), and the type or level of merchandise offered.

Figure 5.1 illustrates the prestige approach in an institutional ad for Barney's. The message for the store's target customer is that the Giorgio Armani Couture Collection is now available and that Barney's has it exclusively—"Unavailable to everyone but Barney's." The small print can be categorized as policy, since it lists the store's location, hours, services ("Free alterations. Free parking."), and information about conditions of sale ("We honor the American Express Card, Master Card, VISA. And, of course, your Barney's card."). Communicating store policy, however, is not the main objective of this ad.

You will note that the merchandise takes a back seat to the institutional message. There is no copy describing it, and the photo does not show the merchandise clearly. Barney's is not attempting to sell an Armani outfit—it is selling the store's image.

Although we are given no information about her, the reader can judge the woman in the photograph to be important, elusive, and rich. Hounded by paparazzi and protected by a bodyguard, she is hurriedly arriving—and is "unavailable." The movement in the photograph conveys a sense of urgency to the reader. The subliminal message of the ad is directed at the Armani customer; the message is that the Couture Collection has arrived, and Barney's is the only one who has it.

The Hills ad (Figure 5.2) is an institutional ad aimed at a very different customer. The intent of the ad is a message regarding the store's conditions of sale policy and the resulting benefits for the Hills customer. By not offering credit, Hills tells its audience it is able to offer low prices (…you don't get the costs of credit in our everyday low prices. That's a difference you'll feel right away.") The ad uses a reverse snob-appeal approach ("For those people who will charge this Christmas, and completely forget about the costly dangers of credit cards, get ready. There will be plenty of bills to remind you come February.")

The Giorgio Armani Couture Collection. Unavailable to everyone but Barney's.

Figure 5.1

Prestige and exclusivity are the messages in this institutional ad.
Courtesy of *Retail Ad Week* magazine.

Figure 5.2

This policy ad outlines the store's conditions of sale and the resulting benefits for its customers. Courtesy of *Retail Ad Week* magazine.

Neiman Marcus used a humorous approach in an institutional ad which ran prior to the opening of its first store in the Northeast (Figure 5.3). Since many of the prospective customers in the new market area only had been exposed to the store through its Christmas catalog, famous for its expensive fantasy items, the ad told the reader that N-M offers merchandise within his or her reach. This institutional ad is noteworthy since it is attempting to amend the prestigious reputation already enjoyed by Neiman Marcus to widen the store's customer base.

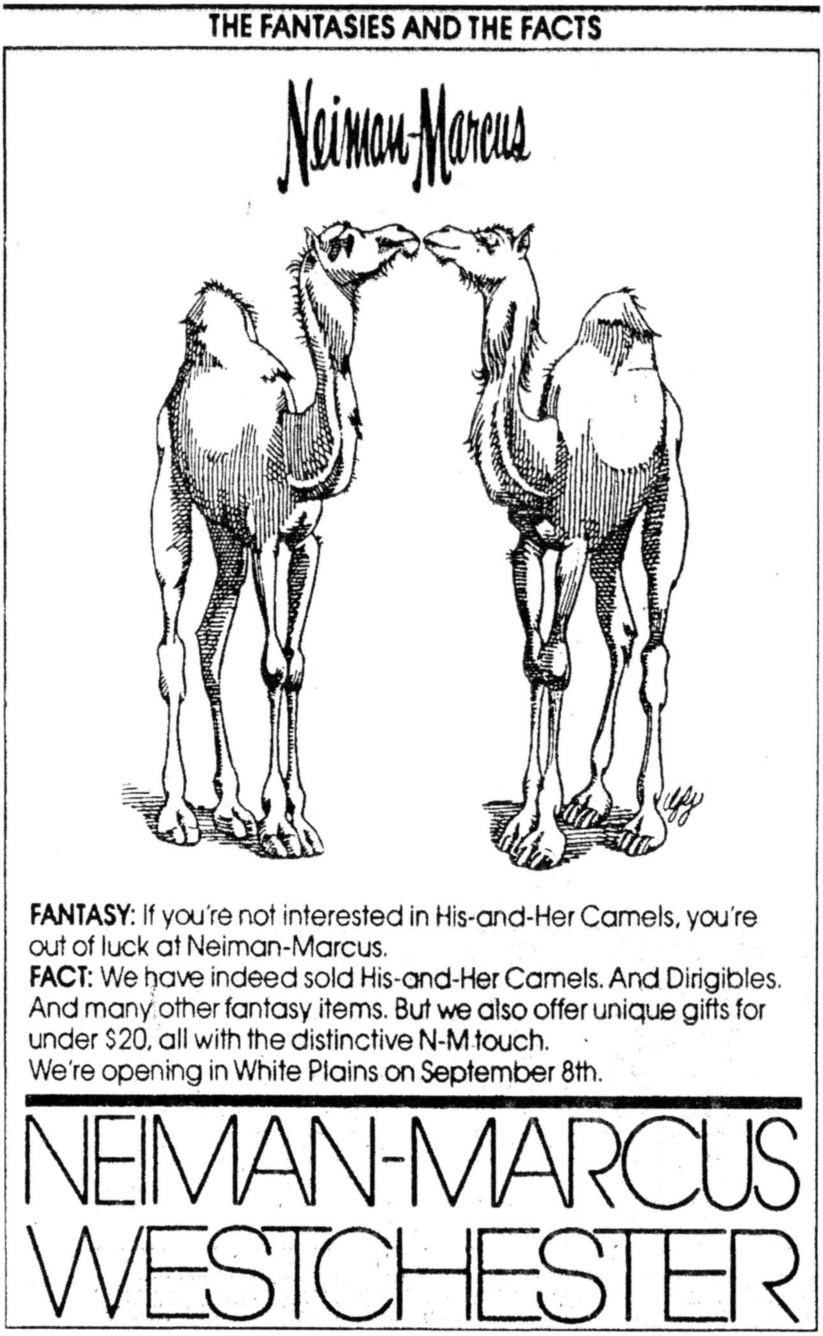

THE FANTASIES AND THE FACTS

Neiman-Marcus

FANTASY: If you're not interested in His-and-Her Camels, you're out of luck at Neiman-Marcus.

FACT: We have indeed sold His-and-Her Camels. And Dirigibles. And many other fantasy items. But we also offer unique gifts for under $20, all with the distinctive N-M touch.

We're opening in White Plains on September 8th.

NEIMAN-MARCUS
WESTCHESTER

Figure 5.3

This institutional ad was used to change the store's image with its new prospective customers. Courtesy of *Retail Ad Week* magazine.

Rich's used the prestige institutional in Figure 5.4 to cleverly convey their vast array of customer services. The use of white space (more about that in Chapter 7) catches the eye. The reader then registers that the drawing is a file drawer. The "headline" on the file drawer ("Rich's Penelope Penn...your shopping organizer") is a whisper by headline standards and serves to draw the reader in. The copy ("...and let Penelope Penn file away your shopping dilemmas") continues to drive home the theme of the ad while the individual folders in the drawer communicate the various services the store offers its customers.

Retailers also spend advertising dollars on messages that have nothing to do with the store, its services, or its merchandise. These institutional messages are designed to build respect for the store, to encourage its image as an active, contributing member of the community. Directed at the mind and heart of the reader, the *good-neighbor ad* message is current, newsworthy, and often powerful. By addressing the concerns currently on its customers' minds, the store is saying to its target customers, "Your concerns are our concerns." The return on the money invested in the good-neighbor ad is long term; the goal of the good-neighbor ad is to affect the store's image.

The topic of this type of institutional ad could be civic, like Lord & Taylor's appeal to vote in Figure 5.5, or a salute to a worthy cause such as the American Red Cross. It could be prompted by a happy event, such as Filene's congratulatory ad addressed to the Celtics in Figure 5.6, or an accomplishment of national significance like a "first" in our national space program. It could also, of course, be prompted by tragedy.

No matter what the topic, the underlying message that the store is trying to convey with this type of institutional ad is that it is more than a business enterprise.

Product Advertising

The lion's share of a store's advertising budget is spent on product advertising. In order for the store to do business, it must convey information about the goods it is offering for sale. Another term used to describe this type of advertising is *promotional* because it promotes the selling of merchandise.

In general terms, product advertising can be classified by the following conditions of sale:

- Regular price
- Special price
- Clearance
- Mail order

Regular-price ads are the most common ad type. The bulk of the store's advertising during a given season centers on the merchandise offered at regular price.

Figure 5.4

This simple institutional ad conveys a lot about the personalized service Rich's offers its customers. Surrounded by white space, the drawing of a file drawer and file folders arrests the eye and carrys out the theme of the ad—Rich's shopping organizer. Courtesy of *Retail Ad Week* magazine.

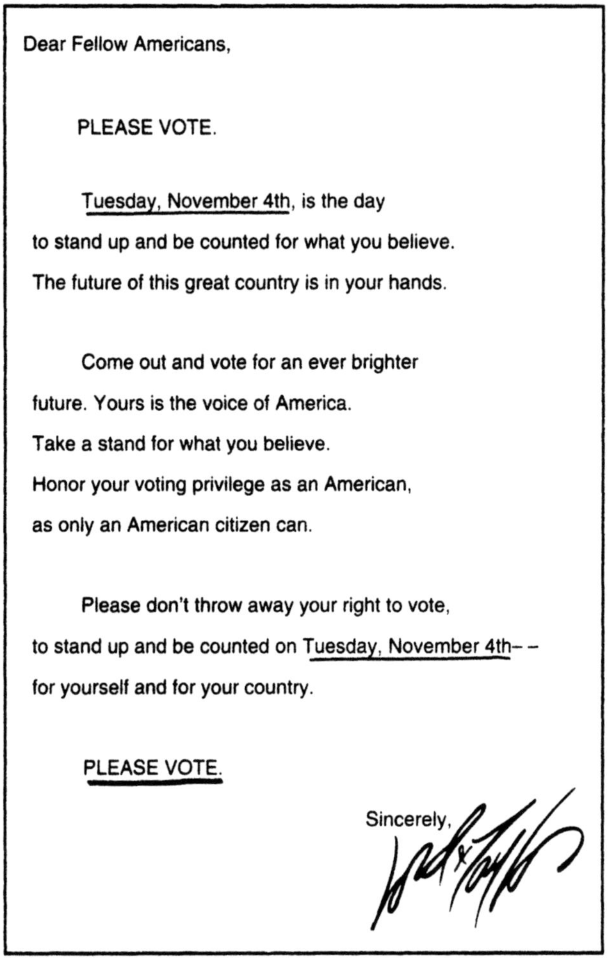

Dear Fellow Americans,

PLEASE VOTE.

Tuesday, November 4th, is the day
to stand up and be counted for what you believe.
The future of this great country is in your hands.

Come out and vote for an ever brighter
future. Yours is the voice of America.
Take a stand for what you believe.
Honor your voting privilege as an American,
as only an American citizen can.

Please don't throw away your right to vote,
to stand up and be counted on Tuesday, November 4th– –
for yourself and for your country.

PLEASE VOTE.

Sincerely,

Figure 5.5

This institutional ad is a classic civic ad. Lord & Taylor's open letter addressed to "Dear Fellow Americans" makes a strong case for voting and tells its readers that Lord & Taylor is more than a store—it is a concerned member of the community. Courtesy of *Retail Ad Week* magazine.

These promotional ads attempt to sell the customer on the benefits of the merchandise currently offered.

The form and style of a regular-price ad is dictated by the merchandise, the image the store wishes to project, and the intended customer the message has been designed to reach.

If, for instance, the main selling benefit of the advertised merchandise is easy care, the ad copy would concentrate on this attribute, addressing the fiber content, care instructions, and the fact that the garment would travel wrinkle-free. Ad copy such as "This inexpensive dress will take you from the office to that special dinner date" is aimed at a working woman who watches her clothing budget.

Regular-price ads commonly contain information about the colors and sizes available and the price of the advertised merchandise. This is not always the case, for—and it bears repeating—the ad copy is determined by what is advertised, who is sending the message, and the customer for whom the message is intended.

Figure 5.6

When the Celtics won their 14th NBA Championship, Filene's joined in the celebration with this "Light Up, Boston" institutional ad. Courtesy of *Retail Ad Week* magazine.

Figure 5.7 is a regular-price ad, but you will note that no price is mentioned, nor are the sizes. The ad, in fact, is intended to sell more than the dress featured—it is really selling the whole Givenchy collection available at Bergdorf Goodman's Givenchy Nouvelle Boutique.

Figure 5.8 is a regular-price ad with strong institutional ad overtones. The artwork of the ad does not feature the merchandise the store offers; the copy contains no specific merchandise or price information. But the ad is clearly in the regular-price category because the copy, which takes the form of a response to a customer's "comment," mentions fashion items of the season. The ad is also institutional since the copy of the ad creates an image of the store. This is a retailer with the merchandise selection, customized personal service ("Why not bring in a few of the things you'll be travelling with and we'll help you put those outfits together."), and price points ("I save you money.") targeted to a traveling working woman on a budget.

HUBERT DE GIVENCHY'S SILK CHIFFON STRIPES
WITH A TWIST FOR EVENING, IN ROYAL BLUE AND YELLOW,
FROM A COLLECTION DEVOTED TO BEAUTY. SPIRITED
DRESSES, NEW-PROPORTION COATS, CLASSIC SUITS.
GIVENCHY NOUVELLE BOUTIQUE, SECOND FLOOR

BERGDORF GOODMAN

ON THE PLAZA IN NEW YORK • 754 FIFTH AVENUE

Figure 5.7
Elegant artwork sets the mood for this regular-price ad. Note the
interesting device: the woman seated in front of a mirror allows the
reader a view of the back of the dress. Courtesy of *Retail Ad Week*
magazine.

Special-price ads are used by a store to build store traffic and sales. The merchandise offered may be a special purchase; that is, the retailer paid less than normal for the merchandise and is passing the savings on to the customer. The special-price ad is also used when the retailer is taking a temporary markdown on
regular merchandise. It has become increasingly common for fashion retailers to
offer merchandise at a "before-the-season price." These special-price ads serve to

"I'm going East on business and I need a few good looking Put-Togethers that won't break the bank."

Can do, Ms. Neill. That's what my store's all about. Put- togethers. Wear that same jacket to dinner over a fresh silk blouse. A new skirt or French pants to go with that other jacket? That's where we shine.

Why not bring a few of the things you'll be travelling with and we'll help you put those outfits together.

You'll find carefully selected, lovingly edited collections of fine tailored sportswear coordinates, two piece silk dressing, imported blouses, pretty tops, skirts, pants, stretch jeans, and much more. Good things to work with the good things you already own. So you don't have to take a steamer trunk with you.

As for breaking the bank, one other very important fact about my store: I save you money.

Women's Haberdashery

Where The Smart Money Shops

14852 Ventura Blvd.   Sherman Oaks   986-8518
Just East of Kester
Hours 10-5:30,   Visa and Mastercharge
Sizes 4-14

Figure 5.8

The conversational style of this regular-price ad speaks directly to the target customer, "answering" her needs and concerns. This ad is also institutional; its emphasis on personalized service communicates the character and style of the store. Courtesy of *Retail Ad Week* magazine.

stimulate demand for just-arrived merchandise, and give the retailer an early reading on what will be best sellers for the store, providing the opportunity for placing reorders, or adjusting existing orders with vendors.

The previously mentioned loss-leader ad is a type of special-price ad. The store sacrifices the profit margin on one item (thus the name) to get customers into the store. The theory is that the increased store traffic and resulting sales storewide offset the loss.

Special-price ads are often utilized at traditional gift-giving holidays. Again, some of the profit margin is sacrificed in order to attract additional business. And, when retail business has slowed, special-price ads act as a catalyst to get customers back into the store.

Because they are designed to build store traffic and boost sales, special-price ads usually have a time limit on them. The headline in Figure 5.9 is the time limit—"10 DAYS ONLY," which is used to motivate the reader to immediate action.

Figure 5.9

Special-price ads motivate customers to come into the store, increasing traffic and storewide sales. Courtesy of *Retail Ad Week* magazine.

Clearance ads are most commonly used at the end of a selling season when a retailer must clear out the stock to make room for the new merchandise on order. Clearance ads are also used during a season when slow-moving merchandise needs a boost. While the word "clearance" is often used, it is not needed to qualify the ad as a clearance ad.

The ad in Figure 5.10 virtually shouts clearance bargains to the reader without using the word. The artwork (empty hangars), the large centered headline, and copy all let the reader know that merchandise is priced to move, translating into real savings for the customer.

Mail-order ads offer merchandise through a nonstore condition of sale. (Don't confuse this category with mail-order catalog business, which we will examine later.)

Retailers offer merchandise through mail-order ads when there is no room for the merchandise on the *selling floor* or as an alternative, convenient way for the customer to purchase merchandise available at the store. Mail-order ads appear in newspapers and magazines and are also sent through the mail, either as a stand alone piece or as an insert into the customer's charge bill. Retailers often use mail-order ads to increase the customer base of the store, since they reach customers who would not physically come to the location to purchase the advertised merchandise. For example, mail-order ads enable the retailer to reach the increased number of working women who can no longer shop during the day.

CLASSIFYING ADVERTISING BY MERCHANDISE

While all retail advertising can be classified by the condition of sale, a more definitive classification for promotional advertising is by the type and amount of merchandise featured in the ad. This classification gives a clearer picture of what the ad was intended to do.

The *single-item ad* concentrates on one unit of merchandise, selling the benefits of that one item to the consumer. Jump ahead and take a peak at the ad for the Burberrys trench coat in Figure 5.18. The only item—and the purpose for the ad—is "a seasonless, timeless investment in coating."—the Burberrys trench.

A *tonnage ad* is a special type of single-item ad. The retailer's intent with the tonnage ad is to sell large quantities of the item.

There are several clues that the JCPenney ad in Figure 5.11 is a tonnage ad. The first can be found in the headlines. "See you later, alligator" indicates that JCPenney intends to market a private label shirt—The Fox—to compete against and capture some of the business of the popular best-seller—Izod's knit shirt with the alligator insignia. The second headline, "The same fit, comfort, quality, looks, and easy-care fabric as well as the well-known knit," all but names the competitor JCPenney is targeting.

Since tonnage ads usually offer merchandise at an attractive price, "at dollars less" is a second, important clue. The price is further emphasized by putting the word "*Only*" in larger type. Even if the reader does not know the price of the Izod shirt, he or she now knows that The Fox will cost less for the same look.

Today our sale is finished.

OPEN SUNDAY 12-5
FINAL MARKDOWNS

This opportunity comes only one day in the entire year. Our very special downtown shop is going on vacation tomorrow. (When we re-open Monday, July 27th, our hangers will hold our spectacular new fall fashions).

This is your last chance to fill your closet with next year's fashions at last year's prices. Reductions as much as 75% (and more). How can you resist?

24™

The Twenty Four Collection
24 street at n e second avenue
576-6424

Figure 5.10

Clearance ads are intended to move the remainder of the season's stock to make room for new merchandise. Courtesy of *Retail Ad Week* magazine.

Figure 5.11

The humorous headline on this tonnage ad is designed to catch the reader's eye. The shirt is available at all large stores, with the men's shirt additionally available through the catalog, indicating that JCPenney plans to sell a large quantity of Fox shirts. Courtesy of *Retail Ad Week* magazine.

Availability is another clue to look for in a tonnage ad, both where the item is available and the sizes and colors offered. The copy at the bottom of the ad indicates that The Fox is available "At large JCPenney stores" and that the "Men's shirt (is) also available through the JCPenney Catalog." His Fox is available in six colors in sizes from small to XX-large. Her Fox is offered in Junior sizes, P-S-M-L, and Misses' 32 to 40 in "Basic or fashion colors selected by JCPenney." The store is targeting a wide range of customers with this private label shirt.

Another merchandise classification for retail advertising is the *assortment ad.* As the name indicates, the assortment ad features more than one item. The assortment ad takes several forms: omnibus, line promotion, related item, and departmentalized.

The *omnibus ad* is a storewide ad featuring items from a variety of departments. The overall purpose of this ad is to generate store traffic. The omnibus ad stretches the advertising dollar since the target audience is widened—there is more offered so there is an opportunity to reach a wider customer audience. This type of assortment ad is a strong candidate for a storewide sale since it allows the retailer to convey information about more items that are on sale to the reader. A

Figure 5.12

Prange's offers suggestions for the "What do I get him/her this year?" question in this omnibus assortment ad for Valentine's Day. By presenting merchandise from several departments, the store is selling the variety it has to offer. Courtesy of *Retail Ad Week* magazine.

gift-giving holiday is another popular time for an omnibus ad. Often used as a vehicle to make gift suggestions, the omnibus ad serves to create the impression that the store offers many alternatives to that particular shopping dilemma. That was Prange's intent in Figure 5.12. By pulling together merchandise from several departments which would be an appropriate Valentine's Day gift for men and women, Prange's ad appealed to and reached a wider audience.

A *line-promotion ad* presents a classification of merchandise and features the low end, middle, and top-of-the-line in that classification. This type of ad is used

Figure 5.13

This line-promotion ad conveys that the store believes in the shawl as a fashion item and has stocked it in several price points. It also enables the store to show that the item can be worn in a variety of ways. Courtesy of *Retail Ad Week* magazine.

to reach more customers in the market and to communicate the range of price points the store offers.

When used for a fashion item, the line-promotion ad allows the retailer to convey the importance of the fashion trend and to educate the consumer as to how the item is worn, as is the case in Figure 5.13. The May Company ad demonstrates to the potential customer, through copy and art, the various ways to wear the shawls the store is offering in three price points: wool voile at $40, solid acrylic at $21, and a border print acrylic at $18.

Figure 5.14

A related-item ad not only tells the reader that the store can meet her wardrobe needs, but supplies instruction on how to combine a new fashion look. Courtesy of *Retail Ad Week* magazine.

Related-item ads are used to promote interdepartment traffic. These ads feature items of merchandise from different departments that complement each other, for example, sneakers in the shoe department and sport socks in the hosiery department. Through a related-item ad, the retailer communicates to the customer that the store is catering to his or her entire wardrobe needs. It is also an opportunity for fashion education; the related-item ad shows the reader how new fashion looks are worn, accessorized, and so on. In Figure 5.14, The Bon demonstrates to the reader how the new shoe shapes fit into the fashion picture.

The *departmentalized ad* concentrates on one department, featuring a variety of merchandise from it. This type of assortment ad establishes a "headquarters" image while widening the appeal of the ad. Through the presentation of the total look, The Denver's ad in Figure 5.15 creates more demand for each of the items featured and shows the variety available in the department.

Theme ads draw their inspiration from a source other than the merchandise presented. If the store is conducting a storewide special event—such as a salute to another country—the store will use that theme in all its advertising. Because a series of ads with the same theme has greater impact, stores often choose an overall theme to introduce the new season's selections.

Figure 5.16 and 5.17 are both theme sale ads. Using an Election Day theme, Stix Baer & Fuller presents sale merchandise from a variety of departments in a neat, readable, and eye-catching format. Of course, this ad would not be as effective if it ran in the middle of the summer; the reason it works is that is draws its theme from a current, top-of-mind event—Election Day. The same can be said of Goldsmith's ad. More than likely, the county fair was in progress when this sale ad ran. The canning jar theme was a topical and eye-catching device to announce a one-day sale in the store's various departments.

Cooperative Advertising

A *co-op ad* is an ad that is paid in part by someone other than the sponsor of the ad. The concept behind co-op advertising is quite simple—shared advertising expense for shared benefits.

Companies in the first two segments of the fashion market spend advertising dollars on national ads to build brand recognition and image for their products at the consumer level. In contributing to the retailer's local advertising by sharing in its cost, these companies ensure that their product's nationally created image is reinforced. In addition, the customer is informed where the product is available for purchase. In essence, co-op advertising is an investment since it helps move merchandise out of the stores to the ultimate customer—the consumer.

For the retailer, co-op dollars stretch the store's advertising budget and can often lend prestige to the store's image because the customer recognizes the brand and has been "sold" on its quality through national advertising.

We already identified the ad in Figure 5.18 as a single-item ad—the only item advertised here (the store itself notwithstanding) is the Burberrys classic trench. It is also classified as a co-op ad.

The prominent display of a brand name is a good indication that an ad is cooperative. In our example, the Burberrys label is the ad's "headline." The line art gives the reader a peak at the famous Burberrys plaid. The retailer is not just advertising a trench coat—it is announcing it has the Burberrys trench traveler. We will take a closer look at co-op advertising in the next chapter.

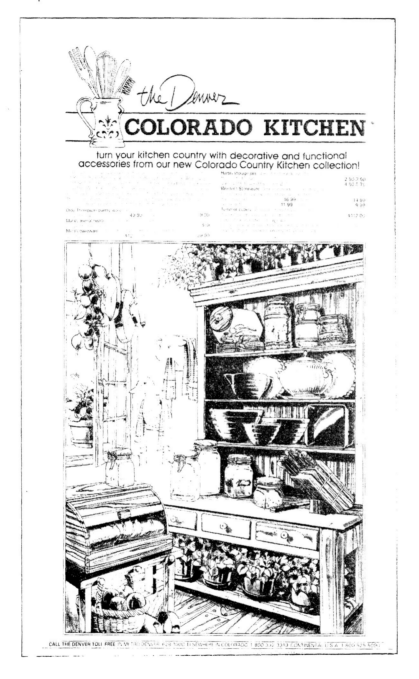

Figure 5.15

A sketch of a well-stocked pantry in this departmentalized ad conveys to the reader that the store has taken a headquarters approach to the collection. Courtesy of *Retail Ad Week* magazine.

Figure 5.16

Using Election Day as its theme, this ad uses a ballot as the vehicle to offer sales merchandise "candidates" from a variety of departments. The reminder to vote is institutional in purpose. Courtesy of *Retail Ad Week* magazine.

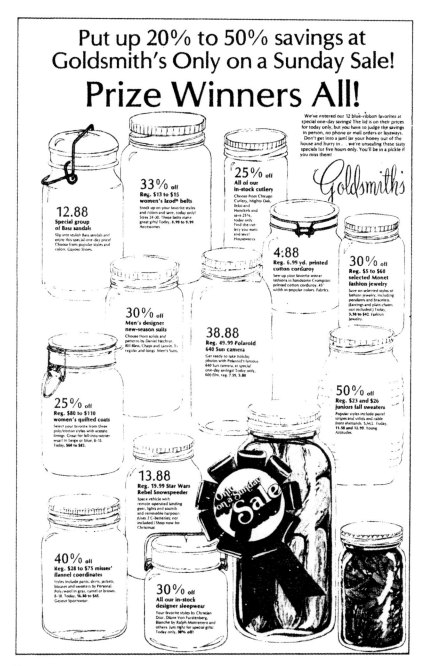

Figure 5.17

This theme ad employs clever copy and artwork to tie together a special-price, one-day sale in unrelated departments. Courtesy of *Retail Ad Week* magazine.

the ⒼS Terrace

'Burberrys'
MADE IN ENGLAND

The classic trench traveler in British tan poplin lined
with famous Burberry plaid. It's a seasonless, timeless investment
in coating, 4 to 16 in the group, 325.00, with Zip-out
blanket lining, 440.00. Because it's as precious as your fur . . .
we'll monogram it for you on the tab for FREE. Allow two weeks.
At the Terrace and the Carriage Shop at NorthPark, and the CS
at Preston Royal, Inwood, and Prestonwood. 214/368-6411.

Figure 5.18

The prestigious Burberrys label serves as the headline in this single-item, co-op ad.
Notice, however, that by offering free monogramming, the store personalized the
ad and gives the customer a reason to purchase the trench at the Terrace and the
Carriage Shop. Courtesy of *Retail Ad Week* magazine.

Summary

Even though retail advertising is categorized as a nonpersonal form of communication, effective retail advertising is personalized in order to reach the target audience. Institutional advertising sells the store itself. Product advertising promotes the goods the store is offering for sale.

Retail ads can be classified by conditions of sale, or by the type and amount of merchandise featured in the ad. One particular ad could belong to several categories. A theme ad, for example, could be a regular-price and an omnibus ad at the same time.

A co-op ad is one that is paid for in part by someone other than the sponsor of the ad. It is an arrangement of shared expense for shared benefits.

Terms for Review

1. Loss-leader ad
2. Institutional advertising
3. Prestige ad
4. Policy ad
5. Good-neighbor ad
6. Promotional ad
7. Regular-price ad
8. Special-price ad
9. Clearance ad
10. Mail-order ad
11. Selling floor
12. Single-item ad
13. Tonnage ad
14. Assortment ad
15. Omnibus ad
16. Line-promotion ad
17. Related-item ad
18. Departmentalized ad
19. Theme ad
20. Co-op ad

Study Review Questions

1. Why does a retailer use a mix of retail ads?
2. What is the ultimate goal of all retail advertising?
3. Why would a retailer spend advertising money for an ad that does not mention merchandise?
4. What is the difference between policy and prestige institutional advertising?
5. What does a good-neighbor ad accomplish for the retailer? Give an example of a current event, either local or national, that would qualify as a theme for this type of institutional ad.
6. What are special-price ads designed to do, and why is there usually a time limit?
7. What are mail-order ads, when are they used, and what are they intended to accomplish?

8. What are the four forms of the assortment ad?
9. When would a retailer use a line-promotion ad and why?
10. What are the shared benefits of co-op advertising?

Case

Thatcher's Department Store is located in a midsized city that serves as the commerce center for the surrounding agricultural region. In addition to the downtown flagship store, Thatcher's has a branch at the new mall off the interstate highway.

In addition to a grain elevator and agriculture market center, the city has several industrial plants and a four-year college and is headquarters for a national insurance company. The college has a football team with a strong local following.

Thatcher's competition includes a smaller department store, a branch of a large discount store chain, and small independent retailers. Thatcher's prides itself on its fashion leadership, good value, and special customer services.

Questions

1. What themes would Thatcher's use for its institutional advertising?
2. Name two local events that would be topical themes for Thatcher's good-neighbor ads.
3. Explain why Thatcher's would use mail-order ads to increase its business.

6

MORE ABOUT CO-OP ADVERTISING

There is a good reason why an entire chapter on cooperative advertising is included in a book on fashion sales promotion. Co-op advertising has become big business and is an important aspect of the sales promotion efforts of today's retailer. No longer a preferential gift or just a sales incentive, co-op advertising has become a planned addition to the retailer's promotion budget, a planned ingredient in the store's communication efforts.

The overall purpose of co-op advertising is to increase sales at the retail level and thus increase sales for the manufacturer or the sponsor of the co-op program. Since co-op advertising helps to move merchandise out of the store, it is a means of increasing marketing efficiency for all involved.

The cooperative advertising practice dates back to before 1900. At that time manufacturers had begun to use national advertising to establish recognition for their brands of merchandise in the consumer market. To reinforce their national advertising campaigns, manufacturers turned to the retailers, who regularly and effectively reached the consumer through local media. The plan was designed for mutual benefit—a cooperative ad would advertise both the manufacturer's product and the retailer's store. If a retailer used the manufacturer's brand name in the advertisement, the manufacturer picked up a portion of the advertising cost.

Without co-op advertising, the manufacturer is forced to depend on the individual retailer's advertising efforts or on national advertising to communicate the benefits of a particular brand to the consumer. National advertising cannot match the force of local advertising in moving merchandise. That is because local advertising not only sells the customer on the benefits of a particular product but tells the customer where it is available.

The origins of co-op advertising can also be traced to a less honorable practice at the beginning of the century. Already under fire for giving large retailers price breaks, some manufacturers used co-op advertising to circumvent regulators.

In most retail operations, it is the buyer's responsibility to research and secure the co-op dollars available to the store. In order to prompt their buyers, stores now include a question about co-op on the store's purchase order. The "Do you offer co-op funds?" line ensures that the buyer will inquire about the availability of a co-op program before leaving the manufacturer's showroom.

It is important that a retailer be aware of available co-op funds. Since many manufacturers factor the cost of co-op advertising into the price of the goods sold to the retailer, the retailer has in effect already paid for the co-op funds. It is a use it or lose it situation. In 1995, it is estimated the U.S. manufacturers and wholesalers will offer more than $15.5 billion in co-op funds. A substantial amount of this co-op money will not be utilized due to lack of attention or misconception about the practice.

The aggressive retailer investigates all available programs, evaluates their value to the store, and utilizes them when appropriate. Co-op advertising represents added revenue for the sales promotion budget. Once used primarily for advertising in newspapers, co-op programs have been broadened to include other media and other sales promotion activities. Since federal regulations ensure that all retailers get equal treatment, co-op programs represent a means for a retailer of any size to increase its exposure with its target audience. The wise and creative use of co-op dollars is another way to set the retailer apart from its competition.

Eligibility

The basis for a co-op program is simple. The store accrues a certain amount of money based on the amount of merchandise purchased from the manufacturer. The retailer has in effect a credit account of co-op dollars upon which to draw. The percentage varies, but between 3 and 5% *accrual* is common in the fashion industry. There is also a specified percentage that the manufacturer/sponsor will pay of the total cost of the advertisement. A 50–50 participation is common, but some programs allow a 100% *bill-back*.

The payment by a manufacturer to a retailer for advertising the manufacturer's product through local media is called *vertical co-op*. To use the co-op funds accrued, a retailer bills the manufacturer, sending proof that a cooperative advertisement has been run. We will examine what constitutes proof later in this chapter.

In the example outlined in Figure 6.1, the co-op program is for a 3% accrual on the store's purchases, with a 50–50 ad participation. In the first example, the store ran an ad costing $600. You will note that even though the store has a co-op credit of $600, the co-op sponsor only reimburses half that amount—leaving a $300 credit in the store's account. When the store runs an ad costing $1,200, the manufacturer reimburses half the cost of the ad, or the full $600 in accrued credit.

Ingredient co-op is money accrued based on the ingredients of the end product. While ingredient co-op is less common at the retail level, you have undoubtedly seen examples of it. When a retailer advertises a garment and specifically mentions the name of the fiber, using the registered trademark, the fiber producer

Co-op program: 3% of purchases/50-50 participation

Anywhere Department Store's purchases during the accural period: $20,000

$20,000 x .03 = $600.

Co-op credit: $600.

AD COST	REIMBURSEMENT	REMAINING CREDIT
$ 600	$ 300	$ 300
$1,200	$ 600	$ 0

Figure 6.1

Co-op advertising is based on credit accrued and on the percentage of participation.

is contributing in some way to the cost of the ad. In this way, the fiber producer has helped move merchandise out of the store, reinforced its own national advertising efforts, and, through the domino effect, increased its own sales and profits.

Figure 6.2 is an example of an ingredient co-op ad. The registered trademark of the fabric produced by Milliken & Co.—VISA—appears in two places in the ad. You will notice that the Visa name overshadows the garment manufacturer's name in the ad.

Advantages and Disadvantages

The co-op practice in this country has its good points and its bad for all parties involved. It is an expensive undertaking for the sponsor, and often a red-tape nightmare for the recipient. On the plus side, exposure through the local media does help sell the manufacturer's product, and the retailer does benefit from the increase exposure—the co-op money enables the retailer to stretch the advertising budget and increase advertising. At its best, co-op advertising greases the distribution system; it moves merchandise to the ultimate customer—the consumer.

Proponents of the practice see a co-op program as a valuable selling tool. A co-op program is viewed as an incentive to induce retailers to purchase and advertise the manufacturer's product. The more advertising a retailer does, the greater the sales, so the practice serves to pull goods through the distribution system. Manufacturers then benefit from the increased sales activity. Co-op advertising can be generally described as an investment—a means to increase sales and turn extra profits for both the sponsor and recipient.

Figure 6.2

This co-op ad, which used the registered trademark VISA in two places, was paid for, in part, by the company that produces the fabric—Milliken Co. Courtesy of *Retail Ad Week* magazine.

In addition to stretching the retailer's promotion budget, the co-op practice also serves to stretch the manufacturer's advertising budget. National advertising costs 60% more than local advertising. The practice of charging less for local advertising began years ago to protect local merchants and to encourage their use of the local media. The manufacturer can, through co-op programs, gain increased exposure for less money. It is, in effect, getting its ads inserted in local media at the local rates.

Critics of the practice contend that co-op programs are largely a waste of money for the manufacturer, that the bulk of the advertising conducted with co-op dollars is inappropriate to its business needs. Since retailers have come to expect co-op money to supplement the store's sales promotion budget, critics characterize co-op programs as a form of extortion. The manufacturer has no choice in the matter; in order to stay competitive, a co-op program is a necessary evil of doing business. The manufacturer is portrayed as a victim of a program of ever-increasing size, escalating costs, and widespread abuses.

Some retailers do abuse the programs. When a store charges back a *vendor rate*, it is charging the sponsor the rate listed on the medium's rate card. Sometimes, however, the store does not pay the full rate for the ad, since it is common practice to grant a frequent advertiser a volume discount. Other fraudulent practices include resubmitting the same ad for reimbursement or charging one manufacturer disproportionately for an ad that advertised several brands of merchandise.

Not all abuse is intentional. Inappropriate charge-backs to the sponsor of a co-op program are often a function of how the medium issues an invoice or how it keep its accounts.

For example, a radio station offers a retailer a two-for-one trade deal. The retailer trades goods worth $1,000 at retail for $2,000 worth of advertising time. The invoice that the station provides the retailer as proof of the transaction reads $2,000. But the actual cost to the retailer was $500—the wholesale cost of the merchandise. The unfortunate co-op sponsor—who has agreed to participate in a 50–50 co-op program—pays $1,000, half of the $2,000, instead of $250, half of $500.

To prevent abuses, many sponsors use *audit bureaus* to check retailers' claims. The bureau knows the time and space costs in a given market area and is aware of the volume rates a retailer has earned. Computerized systems help catch duplicate claims, honest errors, or calculated mistakes. The bureaus have the personnel to administer and monitor the co-op program and, depending on the level of service the manufacturer contracts for, can issue marketing reports and pay the store claims.

Many of the sponsors of co-op programs supply the retailer with ads. These ready-to-use ads are sophisticated efforts prepared by the sponsor's advertising agency. The ability to drop the store logo into a prepared mat for print or to tag on the store's name in a broadcast commercial is especially important to the small retailer, but even a large retailer can save staff time and money by utilizing the service.

On the surface, the co-op practice is a bargain the retailer should take advantage of. Co-op programs provide extra money that stretches the store's own sales promotion budget, increasing the store's exposure without increasing the expense. Retailers are able to defray the costs of major storewide promotions by combining the co-op dollars from several sponsors. This assistance enables the store to undertake more sophisticated or extensive promotions than its own budget would allow. Such applications also enable the retailer to defray the promotional costs for merchandise or activities not covered by a co-op program.

But with this extra help comes extra paperwork. The onus is on the store to keep track of the co-op money due it. In order to get reimbursed for the expenditures, the store must supply the sponsor with proof. Complicated requirements and inconsistency from one program to another make the administrative aspect of co-op programs a burden. Since each sponsor can dictate the terms of agreement, this is an uncontrolled expense for the retailer. The paperwork involved in administrating the program cuts into the "profit" of the co-op practice. To counter this problem, representatives from the media can assist the retailer; using the vendor's account number, the newspaper representative, for example, will determine all the important elements of the co-op program for the retailer.

Taking advantage of a co-op program is not always in the best interest of the store. The brand name may not fit the image the store wishes to project, or the supplied ads may not enhance the image of the store. Since the ad agency prepared the ads to feature the manufacturer and the product, the retailer's best interests may not be served. Remember, no matter what the topic of the ad, the overriding function of all retail advertising is to sell the store. Prepared ads often diminish the impact of the store name and identification. By the same token, excessive sponsor requirements may diminish store impact. Having to mention the sponsor's name five times, for example, leaves little space for the store's personalized message.

Finally, a liberal co-op program may be a mask for inferior merchandise. While many retailers miss the opportunity afforded by co-op programs, there are cases of overzealous retail management. In an attempt to get as much additional money as possible, they are guilty of applying pressure to the buyers to purchase goods from suppliers that offer co-op over those who do not. There is an obvious danger in this approach; while increased exposure does increase sales, no amount of advertising can compensate for inferior quality.

Federal Rulings

In its infancy, co-op was used by some as a means of offering discriminatory price breaks to large retail customers. The passage of the Robinson-Patman Act in 1936 made it illegal to use co-op advertising money as a means of preferential treatment. This basic regulatory act outlines the responsibilities of all parties involved in the process of offering and utilizing co-op funds. Among other points, the act made it illegal to offer co-op money unless the program is extended to all retailers on "proportionally equal terms." The law requires that a customer purchasing $1,000,000 worth of merchandise be granted exactly double that which is offered to a $500,000 customer.

The competition division of the Federal Trade Commission is the regulatory agency for co-op programs. The FTC has guidelines to which the sponsor and user of co-op money must adhere. The following topics are covered in the guidelines:

- "Need for plan"—the seller must have a written plan including all specifications.
- "Proportionally equal terms"—services and payments must be made available equally to all competing customers.
- "Seller's duty to inform"—co-op sponsors must inform all their customers of the program regardless of the size of the store or the size of the purchase.
- "Availability to all competing customers"—the seller cannot pick and choose who will be entitled to the co-op funds.
- "Need to understand terms"—the onus is on the sponsor to make sure the retailer understands the terms of agreement, thus eliminating forfeits due to ignorance.
- "Checking customer's use of payment"—this eliminates preferential treatment and helps regulate retailer abuse.
- "Competing customers"—all retailers in competing markets must be treated on a fair and impartial basis.

These regulatory rules are applicable to both dealer and retailer, making the retailer equally responsible for following and adhering to the guidelines.

The Co-op Advertising Agreement

You may have noticed that the FTC regulations do not specify *what* the sponsor of co-op programs may offer. The regulations only ensure that whatever is offered is extended equally to all retailers.

Although nearly every manufacturer or supplier has some form of co-op program, there is wide variance in the scope and requirements of the programs.

A *manufacturer co-op agreement* is the starting point when entering a co-op program. It is a contract between the manufacturer and the store. In the instance where the manufacturer doesn't have a co-op agreement, the store can create an agreement like the one in Figure 6.3. Or, as mentioned earlier, representatives from the various media can assist the retailer in gathering co-op specifications.

The manufacturer's agreement has several practical purposes. Normally signed before the ad runs, it serves as notice to the manufacturer that the store intends to utilize the co-op program. This notice alerts the manufacturer that the store's accrual credit should be tracked. Perhaps more important, the manufacturer's agreement outlines the specifications for that particular co-op program. All the special rules, requirements, and limitations must be accepted by the retailer. The retailer should scrutinize the manufacturer's agreement before signing to be sure that the store can or wants to meet all the requirements. It is at the point of

Anyplace Department Stores

Co-op Advertising Information Request

Date: _____

Manufacturer's Name _____

Home Office Address _____
_____
_____

1. Does your company offer a co-op ad allowance? _____

2. What is the basis for accural of co-op funds? _____

3. What is the time period the accrual is based on? _____

4. Based on my purchases, how much ad allowance do I have
available to spend? _____

5. On what basis is your co-op program based --50/50, 75/25, 100%,
or a fixed line rate basis? _____

6. Are there time limits when the ad must appear? _____

7. What "proof of performance" does your co-op plan require?
_____
_____

8. How soon after the an ad appears must we submit "proof of performance"
and where do we submit our reimbursement claim?
_____
_____

9. Please list any special requirements for compliance.
_____
_____
_____

This form has been completed by: Name: _____

Title: _____

Anyplace Department Store Buyer: Phone: _____

Figure 6.3

The retailer can send a form like this to get all the proper information about the manufacturer's co-op program.

signing the agreement that the retailer should decide if the co-op program is in the store's best interest. The manufacturer, after all, has a reason for offering the co-op money. The retailer must realize what the program is designed to accomplish and whether the store should participate. Since the store's promotion budget and promotional activities are planned with the co-op money in mind, overlooking the "fine print" restrictions of the contract could prove costly.

No matter how diverse the agreements are, all can be reduced to five basic elements.

1. *Timing*. Each co-op program has timing factors. One timing factor affects what will qualify for the accrual of credit. In other words, at what point during the selling season do store purchases qualify the store for co-op money? Other timing factors include when the advertisement can run, when the reimbursement claims must be made, and the period during which the accrual credit must be spent. The retailer should be aware of special provisions that allow funds to be carried over to the next season or allow the credit fund to be increased.

2. *Accrual*. Accrual is the co-op money earned by the store based on a percentage of the purchases it makes. A time limit is usually specified for the accrual period. Other specifications the retailer should watch for include the basis for qualification for the program and exactly how the store earns co-op money. Another important factor is how the store will be notified of the amount in the accrual fund.

3. *Participation*. The participation portion of the agreement spells out exactly what percentage of the retailer's promotional costs are paid by the co-op sponsor. In Figure 6.1, the manufacturer had a 50% participation agreement. The participation percentage could be 50%, 75%, or as high as 100%. Some agreements outline fixed rates for the different media. A *fixed line rate*, for example, is the amount the sponsor will pay for a line of newspaper advertising, no matter what the paper bills the store.

4. *Special requirements*. It is in this section that the sponsor guidelines for promoting the product are delineated. What the advertising must be like in order to qualify for the funds, what products may be advertised, and any limitations for the advertisement are outlined. The requirements for size, length, or frequency are discussed, as is the types of media that may be used, whether or not the sponsor requires advance approval of the advertisement, how the sponsor logo must be used in the ad, and whether the sponsor will allow the store to include competitive products in the ad. This section may also contain requirements for notification of changes in or termination of the co-op program or contact.

5. *Reimbursement*. The sponsor of the co-op program returns money to the retailer after receiving proof that all the requirements of the agreement are met. The reimbursement section of the contract spells out what documentation is needed, how the retailer's claim should be submitted, and how the retailer is paid.

Reimbursement Documentation

The sponsor of the co-op program often provides a form to be used by the retailer when filing a claim for co-op reimbursement. Again, the representative from the media used for the ad may be able to help the retailer in filing for reimbursement, and there are outside third-party companies that will perform this task for a fee. The basic information needed for filing a claim includes:

- Where the ad ran
- When the ad ran
- The space used in column inches
- The net rate per inch
- The total cost of the ad
- The vendor's co-op cost

Most sponsors require third-party or medium-provided evidence of the costs incurred. This practice serves to cut down on fraudulent claims and gives the sponsor documentation of the dollars paid out for co-op funds. The documentation is different from one medium to another, but the basic requirement is evidence of what the advertisement consisted of and what the retailer paid for it.

Newspaper.   The newspaper provides the store with an invoice for the ad space and a full-page *tearsheet*. Nothing less than a full-page tearsheet will prove when and where the ad ran.

Radio.   The station provides an invoice and a script of the ad bearing the Association of National Advertisers/Radio Advertising Bureau Electronic Tearsheet. The electronic tearsheet tells how many times that particular script ran and at what cost.

Television.   An invoice and script bearing the Association of National Advertisers/Television Bureau of Advertising Electronic Tearsheet are provided. Again, the electronic tearsheet is a signed statement placed on the script or storyboard telling how many times that ad ran and at what cost.

Direct mail.   A copy of the mailer is required. If the sponsor agreed to pay printing costs, a copy of the printer's invoice is needed. Some documentation of the distribution costs is required, either postal receipts or invoices from the mailing house.

Special promotions.   When a retailer gets permission from the co-op sponsor to apply co-op money to promotion efforts not covered in the standard agreement, special care should be taken that both parties agree on the documentation. It could be as simple as a photograph of the billboard or a press kit for the store's special event—but it is imperative that there be prior agreement and compliance if the retailer is to be reimbursed.

Retailer-Driven Programs

Retailer-driven programs are an extension of the retailer's regular co-op program. Also known as vendor-supported programs, this is the practice of applying for special funds from a retailer's key vendors for a special promotion. These programs use extra funds, beyond those already generated through co-op programs. This practice benefits both the retailer and the vendor. By subsidizing a special event at the retail level, the vendor is assisting the retailer in moving product through the retail outlet to the ultimate customer. The partnership increases sales and profit for both the retailer and the vendor, increases visibility for the vendor's product, and generates traffic and sales at the store.

We will examine the different types of special events that retailers conduct in Chapter 14. To secure extra support from its vendors, the retailer demonstrates a special need, such as a grand opening, special sale, or new product introduction. The retailer presents a plan that includes increased advertising exposure and increased planned sales.

Media Involvement

We have discussed the benefits co-op provides the retailer and the sponsor of the program. Another group benefiting from co-op programs is the media.

Co-op programs bring more advertising dollars to the media. While newspapers capture 70–75% of all co-op funds, the other media used for co-op advertising include radio, direct mail, TV, the Yellow Pages, and magazines.

In recent years there has been a shift in co-op programs to allow the increased use of the broadcast media, magazines, and other vehicles. Many manufacturers have broadened media eligibility to include weeklies, preprints, and out-of-home advertising. Television has proven to be a cost-effective method of reaching a store's customers, and stations have attempted to attract more co-op money by supplying kits that can be adapted for co-op advertising, thus decreasing the cost of production for the store.

Another way the media are trying to increase their revenue from co-op funds is to have someone on staff to handle co-op programs. Realizing that much co-op money goes unspent because the programs differ and are often confusing, an increasing number of newspapers, radio and television stations, and magazines have set up special co-op divisions in their ad departments. These special divisions are staffed with people who help a retailer research the store's suppliers for co-op programs, ascertain all the requirements of the individual co-op programs, and assist in filing the proper claim for reimbursement. In some cases, the media co-op division will actually handle the whole claim process, speeding up reimbursements and removing the paperwork burden from the retailer.

Summary

The cooperative advertising practice has become a viable aspect of the retail sales promotion effort. While there are some drawbacks, the practice is largely beneficial to both the sponsor of the program and the participating retailer. An extension of the regular co-op program is the retailer-driven or vendor-supported program, in which extra funds are requested from the vendor by the retailer to apply to special events or promotions. Again, both retailers and vendors benefit from the increased sales and profits generated by the special promotion.

Since co-op funds bring added revenue to the different media utilized, dedicated personnel at the media level assist retailers in implementing co-op programs.

The co-op agreement differs widely from sponsor to sponsor, but can be reduced to five elements: timing, accrual, participation, special requirements, and reimbursement. Federal regulations ensure that all retailers receive equal treatment.

Terms for Review

1. Accrual
2. Bill-back
3. Vertical co-op
4. Ingredient co-op
5. Vendor rate
6. Audit bureau
7. Manufacturer co-op agreement
8. Fixed line rate
9. Tearsheet
10. Retailer-driven programs

Study Review Questions

1. How is co-op advertising a means to increase market efficiency?
2. What are some of the reasons that co-op advertising got off to a slow start?
3. Who is responsible for securing co-op dollars and how are they prompted to do this?
4. How do the proponents of the co-op advertising program view this business practice?
5. How do the critics of the co-op advertising program view this business practice?
6. What are some of the problems that may cause a retailer to turn down co-op money?
7. What did the Robinson-Patman Act of 1936 do?
8. Explain the timing element of a manufacturer's co-op advertising agreement.
9. What is the media doing to try to increase co-op advertising revenue?

Case

You and management decide that elegant, "dressy" jogging suits will be a great Christmas seller. You decide to spend $50,000 of your department's budget on the item and earmark $2,500 for a special advertising effort.

Three manufacturers are offering the item. All other factors affecting your buying decision are the same: price, delivery, colors, quality, and so on. Your choice will be based on the co-op program each is offering.

Manufacturer A has a 5% accrual policy and will pay 30% of the retailer's co-op ad. The accrual is based on an unlimited amount of merchandise purchased; however, the accrual must be used within 90 days.

Manufacturer B has a 4% accrual policy and pays 40% of the retailer's co-op ad. The accrual is paid up to $1 million worth of merchandise purchased. The retailer then has a six-month period to use the credit.

Manufacturer C has a 3% accrual policy and pays 50% of the retailer's co-op ad. The accrual is limited to $100,000 of purchased merchandise, but may be passed from season to season without an expiration date.

Questions

1. Which is the best co-op program for your store?
2. Would your choice be valid if you were a larger store and needed more merchandise?

WHAT IS A GOOD AD?

Whether the intention is to sell high fashion or widgets, the underlying philosophy is the same. In broad terms, the purpose of an advertisement is to sell a product, idea, or service. If the ad fails to do so, big dollar investments and valuable time are lost.

Yet the ad that failed to produce results may have followed all the rulebook principles that should have made it a success. Why then did it fail? In this chapter, we will examine the elements of an ad to determine what it takes to successfully communicate with the ad's target audience.

Figure 7.1 is an example of an ad in which all the elements we will be examining work together to achieve the desired result. It has eye-arresting balance, uses topical copy, and subtly sells the benefits of the product advertised.

Pendleton ran this national ad in *Men's Health, GQ, Outside, Food & Wine, Gourmet,* and *Life* magazines. The placement of the ad in these consumer magazines indicates that the audience for the ad is upscale. The photograph used in the ad, depicting a man in an office setting, further confirms that the ad is aimed at a white-collar audience.

The theme used in the copy of the ad is "current" and therefore captures the intended reader's interest. Major employers throughout the country had begun to relax dress codes for their employees. The topic of casual dress codes, the policies of well-known companies, and speculation of the effect of the trend filled the general press. The ad copy theme is drawn from the then topical "lifestyle" development.

The close-up photo of the Pendleton shirt serves two purposes. It acts as a visual border for the ad and, by showing the shirt in detail, subtly sells the quality the company is famous for. The Pendleton label, lower right, finishes the ad. It acts as the ad's headline, draws the eye to the copy to its left, and sells the quality the brand offers. "Warranted To Be a Pendleton" and "Since 1863" says upscale, quality, and prestige to the targeted reader.

Figure 7.1

Creativity is hard to define, but easy to recognize. This ad has all the elements to make it successful. Courtesy of Pendleton.

Broadly, it can be said that a successful retail ad is one that presents the right merchandise or service at the right time, at the right price, to the right customer. This, of course, presupposes that the retailer has done the marketing homework needed to fully understand just who the store's target customer is. The retailer must also know something about the target customer if the advertising communication is to be effective. The retailer's communication will not get through unless it is of interest to the customer it is intended to reach.

Applying AIDA to Retail Advertising

As we explained in Chapter 1, AIDA is the classic model for selling of all kinds and can be applied to our study of what makes a good retail ad.

ATTRACTING ATTENTION

The first key to the success of any ad, whether it is in print or broadcast, is to attract the target audience's attention. The *broadcast media*, TV and radio, have more options available to attract the attention of the target customer. The element of sound is available to both; visual movement is available to the television ad.

For print, however, the function of attracting the target audience's attention is more complex. Three elements combine to achieve the first task of a successful ad: the ad's *headline, illustration,* and *layout* all serve to attract the reader's eye.

The headline is the featured idea of the print ad and is the primary eye-arrester. The headline tells the "story" of the ad; its major function is to compel the customer to read on. The headline and, if one is present, the subhead help the reader judge whether the message is meant for him or her.

The illustration performs a similar function, telling the reader at a glance the essence of the message being conveyed. Illustrations can be either photographs or line drawings.

The layout of a print ad, or the way the ad is put together, is another factor in attracting attention. The ad's layout helps guide the reader's eye movements so that the ad's important selling points are seen. Figure 7.2 shows a few layout options, but the layout decision is a creative one. It is the answer to the same question that determines the headline and illustration for an ad: What will attract the attention of our target customer?

GENERATING INTEREST

The second task in the AIDA model is to generate interest in the item or service sold. The *copy block* of a print ad or the text of a broadcast ad serves this function.

Sometimes referred to as the body of the ad, this element provides information to the customer whose curiosity has been awakened by the attention-getting

 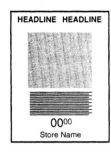

Figure 7.2

Layouts contain five major elements, as shown in these standard layout mock-ups: headline, illustration (represented by solid gray area) copy, price, and store logo. Copyright Newspaper Advertising Bureau, Inc.

elements of headline, illustration, and layout. The body of the ad clarifies the reader's image of what is being offered.

CREATING DESIRE

Persuading the customer that he or she desires the item or service offered is the overall purpose of the advertisement. The job started by the headline and the ad's illustration is now completed by the body of the ad. It contains the major selling points or reasons why the customer should desire the product or service.

OBTAINING ACTION

After the reader is persuaded to desire the product or service, the ad must prompt him or her to action. This is accomplished by listing store locations, telephone numbers, store hours, and convenience services such as free delivery. In the case of a sale ad, a time limit is often given.

More About Layout

We have already explained that the layout or format of an ad helps attract the target customer's attention. In addition, ad layout serves another important function in the retailer's communication with the store's target customer.

The way a retailer presents an ad tells the reader a lot about the store. The layout creates an overall impression on the reader. A retail ad with a large illustration and plenty of *white space* (those areas which are uncovered by type or pictures) tells the reader that the ad is sponsored by a fashion store; the retail ad jammed with type and illustrations gives the impression that the store is offering bargains.

Other elements of layout that convey an impression about the store include the *typeface* used in the ad and the *store logo.* Typeface is the style of type and the size, measured in points. The store logo is the store's business signature.

Retailers strive for consistency in ad layout so that their ads are easily recognized. They establish an ad "look," consisting of the type and size of the illustrations used, the placement of the headlines and store logo, and the typeface used in the ad. This basic format is then repeated for most of the store's advertisements. A standard format makes sense; once a customer is attracted to the store, the retailer wants to make it easy for the customer to locate future messages.

Such is the case in the Henri Bendel ads in Figures 7.3 and 7.4. While the products advertised are different, the two ads utilize the same look; they are easily identifiable to the store's customer. The bottom border of the ads incorporates the store's logo and stripes, a creative tie-in to the store's famous brown and white packaging. Note that in Figure 7.3 the "Bendel's box" is added to the line drawing, balancing the sketch and serving to further identify the store. The border around the ads are also used to "title" the ad; it is where the headline of the ad is found.

The Element of Creativity

We have identified the elements found in successful ads, and the basic functions an ad must achieve to be successful. There is one more crucial factor that must be present for an ad to do its job properly.

Creativity, the way in which the ad is visualized and executed, is vital to its success. Remember, the customer is bombarded with advertising messages daily. Even if the retailer knows who the target customer is and what will appeal to that customer, the message may be lost in the shuffle if the retailer does not present it creatively.

Look again at Figure 7.3. The creative element of moving the line drawing out into the border effectively catches the eye and emphasizes the line drawing. Imagine if the line drawing would have been placed inside the border; it would not have been as dramatic.

Figure 7.3
This ad is aimed at the "significant other" of the store's target customer. It features a Valentine's Day gift idea—a theme carried out through copy and art. Copyright Henri Bendel 1995.

Figure 7.4

While the product advertised is available at other retailers, the style of the ad identifies it as Henri Bendel. Copyright Henri Bendel 1995.

The headline of Figure 7.3 is also creative. "A Perfect Pair" not only refers to the sweater set featured. Since the ad ran in time for Valentine's Day, it is a play on words for that holiday—"The perfect Valentine's Day gift for your very own Sweater Girl."

Even the inclusion of the "Bendel's box" was a creative touch. We already noted that it added balance to the line drawing and helped to further identify the store. But since the ad in Figure 7.3 was aimed at the "significant other" of the Bendel's customer, the box in the ad serves two other purposes. It says "gift," which the reader has in the back of his mind that he better have for the fast-approaching holiday, and while he might not remember his "Sweater Girl's" favorite store by name, the distinctive packaging might ring a bell.

Unfortunately, there are no rules for creativity. But, while it can't be defined by hard-and-fast rules, the absence of creativity is always painfully obvious.

Checklist for a Good Ad

The following checklist is a generalization of what constitutes a good retail advertisement. It is by necessity general: in the final analysis, what works for one store will be disastrous for another. Each store has unique marketing factors that affect the advertising message. The image the store wishes to project, the customer the store wishes to reach, and the competition the store faces all determine what is a "good" ad. In other words, a good ad is one that gets the message to the right consumer and prompts him or her to become a customer of the store. Generally, then, a good ad is one that:

- Captures the reader's/viewer's attention
- Presents benefits to be obtained by buying the product
- Makes honest claims
- Convinces the reader/viewer to shop at the sponsoring store rather than at the competition
- Supports and advances the image the store wishes to project
- Directs the message to the store's target customer
- Urges immediate action
- Has fresh and creative copy
- Speaks directly to the prospective customer, using words like "you" or "yours"
- Presents the information as news
- States specifics, such as size, color, price
- Gives branch locations and phone numbers
- Features timely merchandise
- Is visually uncluttered
- Arrests the reader's eye
- Prominently displays the store's logo

Summary

The underlying purpose of all advertising is to sell a product, idea, or service. To do this, the ad must perform the tasks of the classic selling model AIDA: attract attention, generate interest, create desire, and obtain action. These tasks are accomplished through the basic elements of an ad.

The layout of an ad communicates information about the store to the customer. Once the retailer has decided on a layout that communicates the desired impression, it is used repeatedly to lend consistency to the store's advertising. In this way, the customer recognizes the store's ad by its "look."

The crucial and hard-to-define element in ad presentation is creativity. The creative use of ad elements makes the retailer's ad stand out and increases its chance of reaching the target customer.

Terms for Review

1. Broadcast media
2. Headline
3. Illustration
4. Layout
5. Copy block
6. White space
7. Store logo
8. Typeface

Study Review Questions

1. What is the underlying purpose of all retail advertising?
2. Why does the retailer have to know the store's target audience?
3. What kind of information does the retailer need about the store's target audience?
4. What are the three elements in a print ad that attract a reader's eye?
5. What is the function of an ad headline?
6. What information can a reader gain by looking at the ad's illustration?
7. In terms of attracting the reader's attention, what function does layout perform?
8. What information does that ad's layout convey in terms of store image?
9. Why is creativity important in retail ads?

Case

From the local newspaper, choose two retail ads—one that you feel is a "good" ad and one you feel fails. Remember, the effective ad need not come from a fashion store or a large store. Creativity and effectiveness are not determined by merchandise price points or advertising budgets.

Questions

1. Discuss the use of white space in both ads.
2. How does the good ad attract the reader's eye? Why does the other one fail?
3. What changes could be made to change the ad from a failure to a success?

8 THE BUYER AND THE AD

Without the intensive participation of the buyer, a store's promotional advertising efforts would never succeed. The buyer's involvement with advertising is ongoing, from the initial planning to the follow-up. The merchandise that will be advertised is purchased and merchandised by the buyer; the buyer supplies information during the ad's visualization and production. When the ad breaks, the buyer is responsible for tracking the results that will be useful in future planning.

The Advertising Plan

As we discussed in Chapter 3, the advertising plan maps out a schedule for the entire store, indicating the calendar periods during which advertising will run. Major selling events will be determined at this stage, as well as the ratio of institutional to promotional advertising. A sum of money is appropriated to the advertising plan as a whole, to be divided thereafter among the various divisions of the store.

The advertising plan is next distributed to the divisional merchandise manager (DMM). From it, the DMM derives a divisional plan for the departments under his or her command and proceeds to divide the budget and determine the extent of advertising exposure each department will receive for a six-month period.

The divisional plan contains the following specifics:

- Resources (manufacturers) whose merchandise will be advertised
- Classification of merchandise to be featured
- Volume potential
- Probabilities of reorders
- Cutoff dates for selling

- Markups that will be obtained
- Number of units that will be required
- Timing of the ad in relation to availability of goods, deliveries, and reorders

Buyers from each department contribute important information for the divisional plan. In addition to identifying the classification of merchandise that should be advertised, they are in the best position to decide which resources can assure availability and on-time deliveries and fulfill reorders.

The worksheet in Figure 8.1 is an example of how the divisional plan looks once it has been broken down by department.

The Buyer as a Team Member

In the process of creating an advertisement, the buyer works closely with others in the buying area as well as numerous specialists in nonsales areas. Producing an effective ad is a close-knit effort demanding clear lines of communication between members of a team drawn from many departments in the store. Communication takes the form of detailed written reports, as well as face-to-face meetings with such people as:

1. *Sales promotion director.* All of the store's sales promotion activities are the responsibility of the sales promotion director. This executive, along with staff members, devises and coordinates all the sales promotion programs for the store.
2. *Advertising director.* All advertising in the various media (newspaper, direct mail, television, and radio) comes under the supervision of the advertising director, who is responsible for deriving and implementing an effective advertising program based on the store's master promotional plan. The ads are executed by a staff consisting of a copy chief, copywriters, art director, layout artists, illustrators, and photographers.
3. *Visual merchandising director.* This executive coordinates all of the window and interior displays, based on the store's promotional plans. The visual display staff designs and builds the displays, dresses the mannequins, and in general creates a "theater" in which the merchandise is shown off to the best advantage.
4. *Fashion coordinator.* The fashion office acts as a link between the buyers and the nonsales departments, providing fashion direction for merchandising and accessorizing items in keeping with the store's image.

The buyer's job is much like that of a specialty store owner's. In addition to selecting and purchasing merchandise that will appeal to the store's target customer, the buyer must find and interact with new resources, maintain good business relationships with established resources, obtain cooperative support for advertising, and keep detailed records of sales. The difference, of course, is that the buyer for a large store adheres to a predetermined plan not of his or her own making.

The buyer receives a copy of the divisional advertising schedule indicating the dates for the promotion of the various classifications. From this, the buyer plans ahead to obtain suitable merchandise. In the course of shopping the market, reliable resources will be developed for supplying specially priced items or items that offer good value. The buyer must be attuned to fashion trends and be prepared to know what will be in demand six months to a year ahead. Keeping a finger on the pulse of the fashion market from the point of view of the store's customer is part of the job of merchandising and is essential to maintaining the store's position in the market.

THE ADVERTISING REQUEST FORM

Based on the divisional plan, the buyer issues an advertising request form for each ad assigned to the department. The name for this form varies with each store; it may be referred to as an "advertising copy information sheet" or an "advertising merchandise information form."

The form is submitted to the advertising director and the art department approximately one to two weeks prior to the ad's publication. Its purpose is to give detailed information about the merchandise so that the artists and copywriters can accurately proceed with the visualization of the ad.

The advertising request form generally provides the following information:

- The date the ad will appear, in which medium, and what size the ad will be
- Department number
- Products to be advertised
- Price of items
- Customer benefits and selling features
- Complete description of items (color, style, fabric, etc.)
- Number of units of merchandise expected to be on hand the day the ad runs
- Expected delivery date of the merchandise
- Cooperative advertising information
- The branch stores that will carry the advertised merchandise
- Total retail value of the merchandise
- Signature approval

You will notice that the Macy's advertising request form in Figure 8.2 states "Copy Information: Give all facts customer needs to purchase." The form also asks: "What copy approach should be used? What emphasis in illustration(s)? Why should customer buy items at Macy's?"

SUNDAY	MONDAY	TUESDAY
Depts: C = 20" *F = 25"* **1** 45 Col. in. ad *Lead Item...price* *Item...price* *Item...price* *Item...price*	**2** *Night Opening*	**3**
Depts: E = 25" *D = 15"* **8** 40 Col. in. ad *Lead Item...price* *Item...price* *Item...price* *Item...price*	**9** *Night Opening*	**10**
Depts: A = 30 *F = 25"* **15** 55 Col. in. ad *Lead Item...price* *Item...price* *Item...price*	**16** *Night Opening*	**17**
Depts: G = 10" *B = 10"* **22** *+ co-op = 10"* 30 Col. in. ad *Lead Item...price* *Item...price* *Item...price*	**23** *Night Opening*	**24**
End of Mo. Sale ad *Dept: A = 25"* **29** *G = 10"* *E = 25"* *B = 10" + 10" co-op* 80 Col. in. ad *Sale Item...price* *Sale Item...price* *Sale Item...price*	**30** *2-Day "End of Month" Sale* *Night Opening*	**31** *2-Day "End of Month" Sale*

1 Select goal

Department	Sales Goal	% of Goal		Department	Sales Goal	% of Goal
A	$7,500	25 %			$	%
B	$2,400	8 %			$	%
C	$3,900	13 %			$	%
D	$4,800	16 %			$	%
E	$5,100	17 %			$	%
F	$6,300	21 %			$	%
Sub-total	$30,000	%		Grand total	$30,000	100 %

2 Decide budget

5	% of sales
$1,500	dollars
+ 600	co-op
$2,100	total
$3/col. in.	rate
700	inches

Figure 8.1

This sample worksheet for ad planning illustrates an organized method for keeping up with the many details of a divisional advertising plan. Copyright Newspaper Advertising Bureau, Inc.

WEDNESDAY	THURSDAY	FRIDAY	SATURDAY
"Holiday Sale" ad All Departments 10 Col. inches **4** 70 Col. in. ad Lead Item...price Item...price Item...price Item...price	**5** *Holiday* *Store Open*	**6** *Night Opening*	**7**
11	"Dollar Days Sale" Ad Depts: A = 35" C = 25" **12** D = 20" 80 Col. in. ad Sale Item...price Sale Item...price Item...price	*Payroll Day* **13** *City Wide Dollar Days* *Night Opening*	**14**
18	Depts: A = 25" **19** D = 15" 40 Col. in. ad Sale Item...price Item...price Item...price	*Payroll Day* **20** *Night Opening*	**21**
25	Depts: C = 20" **26** E = 25" Sale→ D = 35" 80 Col. in. ad Sale Item...price Item...price Item...price Item...price	**27** *Night Opening*	**28**

3 **Select promotion**

List each department's monthly sales percentage of total store sales. Then allot equivalent percentages of the month's total advertising. Calculate the linage for each department.

Department	% of Adv	% of Sales	Linage
A	25%	25%	125"
B (plus co-op)	8	6	30"
C (expanded)	13	15	75"
D (overstocked)	16	19	96"
E	17	17	85"
F	12	12	60"
G	9	6	30"
Total	100%	100%	500"

4 **Schedule ads day by day**

Figure 8.2

The purpose of an advertising request form is to provide comprehensive selling information to the advertising department. Courtesy of Macy's.

These questions illustrate the vital role a buyer plays in retail advertising. The buyer is the major source of selling information. Having already purchased the merchandise for the store, the buyer has gone through the reasoning process to determine why it is appropriate for the store's target customer. The buyer has a mental picture of who will buy the merchandise and why. Unless this information is properly conveyed to the advertising department, the ad's message will be incomplete and the communication will not reach the customer the buyer had in mind when purchasing the merchandise.

WHILE THE AD IS IN WORK

The buyer's role extends throughout the process of actualizing the ad. Following approval of the advertising request form, the advertising director confers with the copy chief and the art director to begin work on the ad. Discussions center on the merchandise and how it will be presented. In many cases, the merchandise manager and the buyer will both be called upon to expand on the information already provided on the advertising request form. They might also give a presentation of the actual merchandise in order to provide a better understanding of what the ad should look like.

The copywriter works from the first *rough layout* of the ad and from copy suggestions from the advertising director and the buyer's information form. The information the buyer has supplied is now translated into topical copy that will serve to generate interest and persuade the customer to purchase. Simultaneously, the merchandise is being illustrated, with either a photograph or line drawing.

The *comprehensive layout,* or "comp," with copy text, headlines and subheads, and all other information that is to be included, is submitted to the buyer for revisions and signature approval. At this point, the buyer corrects any mistakes in spelling, prices, or descriptions and evaluates the ad's interpretation and presentation of the selling points of the merchandise.

The comp goes into production, where it is rechecked and approved by the advertising director. Photographs and illustrations are finalized and submitted to the buyer for approval, providing another opportunity for revisions or corrections.

The illustration is then reduced to fit the layout; the type is set, and copy blocks and headlines are pasted into place on the layout.

Proofs are made of the finished layout, and copies are sent both to the buyer and the art department. The entire process takes from ten days to two weeks. Since the advertising department is simultaneously at work producing ads for the many other divisions within the store, the buyer's role as a source of meaningful data and as a coordinator for the ad is crucial.

The buyer must also coordinate department activities to ensure the ad's success. The store's promotional plans often include tie-in window and floor displays to support the ad. The buyer works with the display department to be certain that merchandise is available for display purposes and to aid in its proper presentation

```
┌─────────────────────────────────────────────────────────────────┐
│                                                                   │
│                      REQUEST FOR SIGN                             │
│                                                                   │
│                                                                   │
│   Dept. _____   Date sign required  _____  │
│                                                                   │
│   Window # _____ │
│                                                                   │
│   Interior   (Advertised)      (Not Advertised)                   │
│                                                                   │
│   Item _____ │
│                                                                   │
│   Style # _____  Price _____  Comparative Price _____         │
│                                                                   │
│   Description: Selling points in order of importance.             │
│                                                                   │
│   _____  │
│                                                                   │
│   _____  │
│                                                                   │
│   _____  │
│                                                                   │
│   Colors _____ │
│                                                                   │
│   Sizes _____ │
│                                                                   │
│   Fabric _____ │
│                                                                   │
│   Signature _____  Date _____          │
│                                                                   │
└─────────────────────────────────────────────────────────────────┘
```

Figure 8.3

Before a sign can be created, information must be given to the sign shop on a form like this.

so that when customers respond to the ad, they will find the merchandise as identified. Window, floor, and point-of-purchase displays are important extensions of the department's promotional effort.

Signs may also be needed to provide additional clarification. In such a case, the buyer orders the appropriate signing from the store's sign shop and checks to be sure signs are in place on the day the ad breaks. A form such as the one shown in Figure 8.3 is used to order signs.

To be certain that they are able to serve customers knowledgeably, the buyer alerts the sales staff about the upcoming ad and related displays. Just before an ad runs, "tearsheets" or *press proofs* of the ad are posted in the department for the edification of the salespeople. The buyer may also hold brief meetings in the department to discuss the ad or any problems that may have arisen relating to the merchandise. Tearsheets may also be mounted on poster-sized cards and displayed in high-traffic areas of the store in order to obtain the broadest possible exposure.

Analyzing the Results

Buyers and store management need to evaluate the results of all advertising in order to determine if an ad produced sales. They will ask:

- How well did the ad pull?
- Did sales justify the investment?
- How can we obtain greater response in subsequent ads?

All the factors that affect response will be examined. The most important indicator is the amount of sales in dollars and number of units sold following an ad's appearance. When an ad fails to draw good response, the store searches for reasons. The cause for good or poor results are often difficult to pinpoint because there are many internal and external factors which affect the results.

For example, extreme weather conditions can be a hindrance or a benefit: heavy storms can make travel difficult and keep shoppers at home or attract them to the store in search for shelter; hot sunny days send people to the beaches or, conversely, attract shoppers to air-conditioned stores. Unexpected public events may compete with shopping or create heavier than normal traffic.

Response to the ad may be delayed, thereby increasing the difficulty of measuring the ad's results. If the ad is institutional in nature, an immediate effect on sales cannot be expected. When the more elusive causes over which the store has no control are eliminated, tangible forms of measurements based on department data are applied.

RECORD-KEEPING AND THE ADVERTISING RESULTS FORM

Buyers are required to keep daily records of dollar sales and the quantity of units sold, along with other pertinent data, such as weather conditions. This information is then reported to the advertising department on a printed form so that they may determine the pulling power of the ad. The buyer also records insights and suggestions that would otherwise be lost by the time a similar promotion is conducted. The form generally includes the following facts:

- Department number
- Number of units sold
- Number of stores
- Dollar sales of item advertised
- Total department sales
- Weather conditions
- Display backups
- Number of units of advertised items in stock before and after the ad ran

The buyer files a copy of the advertising results form with tearsheets of the ad for future reference. The information is important for future comparison and to determine the productivity of advertising expenditures. Future investments will be made based on this information.

DETERMINING THE AD'S EFFECT

In the final analysis, the objective for an advertisement is not only to pay for itself but to show a profit. One of the ways to determine this is through a simple arithmetic formula. The cost of space is divided by the gross sales in dollars. The answer gives the cost percentage or the percentage of return yielded by the ad.

For example:

$$\$72 \text{ (cost of space)} \div \$900 \text{ (gross sales)} = .08 \text{ (cost percentage)}$$

The store examines the cost percentage against department sales and all other related factors in order to determine whether an increase or decrease in advertising expenditure is indicated in future planning. The buyer's goal is to produce high turnover and profits for the department. Advertising is necessary to stimulate traffic and produce sales. Thus, it is in the buyer's interest to actively support each phase of advertising and to provide accurate data to the divisional managers and the advertising department.

Summary

The buyer is a pivotal figure in the store's advertising activities, since the support and information provided by the buyer while an ad is in progress are crucial to its success. Based on the divisional plan, the buyer obtains suitable merchandise and arranges for cooperative support from manufacturers. Detailed record-keeping is important every step of the way, and the buyer must keep close watch over all phases of the ad's creation from its initial visualization to final proofs, supplying detailed information and making revisions when necessary. Before and after the ad breaks, the buyer provides in-store support through visual merchandising, signing, and communication with sales personnel. These are some of the usual responsibilities the buyer will have in relation to advertising:

1. Buying the right items and merchandising the advertisement
2. Submission of an advertising request form
3. Revision and approval of layouts and proofs
4. Coordinating activities with the display department and sign shop
5. Maintaining detailed records of number of units sold and department revenue before, during, and after the ad breaks

6. Obtaining tearsheets for posting in the department and for filing with records
7. Alerting sales staff to the advertising schedule
8. Completing the advertising results form

Terms for Review

1. Rough layout
2. Comprehensive layout
3. Press proof

Study Review Questions

1. What information is required of each buyer for the divisional plan?
2. Who does the buyer work with in the process of creating an advertisement?
3. The name for the advertising request form varies from store to store. What is the purpose of this form?
4. Why is the buyer's input so important?
5. Where does the copywriter get the information needed to create copy for an ad?
6. To support the published advertisement, many stores plan tie-ins with what other forms of promotion?
7. What does the buyer do with tearsheets?
8. What is the most important indicator of response to advertising?
9. What information does the advertising department require from the buyer to determine the power of an ad?
10. What is the arithmetic formula to determine the effectiveness of an advertisement?

Case

You are the buyer for Better Dresses. One of your resources has used a newly developed knit fabric for a classic coatdress. The fabric, made of silk and rayon fibers, has a sheen to it and will not wrinkle. The knit is airy and could be worn year-round. You know many of your store's customers are working women, and you decide the dress will appeal to them. The wholesale price is $70, and the manufacturer can deliver your order in mid-January.

Questions

1. Following the example in Figure 8.2, prepare an advertising request form for the advertising department.
2. What is the copy approach for the ad?
3. Why would you want to fill mail or phone orders?

9 NEWSPAPERS: The Number-One Ad Medium

Merchants have been advertising their wares in newspapers since the eighteenth century in this country, and the practice is still going strong. Despite heavy competition from the broadcast media, newspapers prevail as the top advertising medium. Why the continuing appeal?

We are a nation of habitual newspaper readers. The price is right, the paper can be carried and read at will, and it can certainly be said that newspapers are easy to obtain. Aside from home deliveries, which account for the most sales, newspapers can be bought on almost every street corner—at outdoor and indoor stands, in hotel and commercial building lobbies, at subway stations and bus stops, from pay machines, and even from vendors conveniently posted where there are likely to be traffic jams.

Approximately 62% of the total adult population in the United States reads a weekday newspaper, and that percentage jumps to approximately 69% when the Sunday edition is factored in. Demographically, newspaper audiences are better educated, and are found in upper-income households, as illustrated by Figure 9.1.

Since the main objective of a store's advertising program is to reach the greatest number of prospects in a trading area at the lowest cost within the shortest time period, newspaper display advertising is often the answer. Readership is substantial, and the cost remains low in comparison to other media. Additionally, it has been determined that advertising carried in newspapers is regarded as having the authority associated with the press.

Unlike TV and radio, whose advertising message is more or less uninvited by the viewer/listener, newspapers are sought out by the reader, who turns to them not only for the latest news but for the purpose of checking the ads. In fact, as readers we often shop the newspapers before we shop the store. Newspapers are a daily buying guide for virtually every product category.

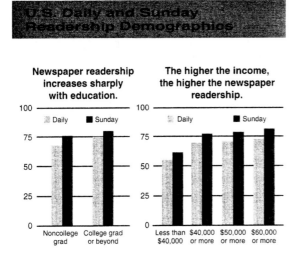

Newspaper readership increases sharply with education.

	Percent Daily	Percent Sunday
College graduate or beyond	75	81
Attended college (1-3 yrs)	68	76
High school graduate	62	70
Attended high school (1-3 yrs)	48	55

The higher the income, the higher the newspaper readership.

Household Income	Percent Daily	Percent Sunday
$60,000 or more	73	81
$50,000 or more	72	79
$40,000 or more	71	78
Less than $40,000	55	63

Source: Simmons Market Research Bureau, Study of Media and Markets, 1993

Figure 9.1

Newspaper readership increases with level of education and household income. Reprinted with permission of the Newspaper Association of America.

Figure 9.2 shows the percentage of advertising revenue captured by newspapers compared to other media. You will note that daily newspapers captured 23.1% of the more than $137 billion of advertising expenditures, and retail ads constituted 12.2%.

Of course, the 12.2% represents retail ads from all types of retail establishments, not just fashion retailers. But to put the numbers into perspective, consider this: during the discussions in the press regarding the merger between Federated Department Stores, Inc., and R. H. Macy and Company, Inc., it was reported that together the two retailing giants spent $390.8 million in advertising, 86% of which was spent on newspaper advertising.

Newspapers are indeed important to fashion sales promotion.

However, while newspaper advertising is a relatively inexpensive and effective means of reaching the store's target customers, most stores believe in maintaining a balanced media program, seeking every opportunity to promote the store and its merchandise.

The Retailer and Newspaper Advertising

Newspaper advertising offers distinct advantages over other media that attract retail advertising. The lower cost of newspaper advertising remains a principal benefit. Newspaper advertising also offers:

Figure 9.2

Newspapers' share of advertising surpasses those of other media. Reprinted with permission of the Newspaper Association of America.

1992 and 1993 Sales and Percentages
(Pie chart represents 1993)

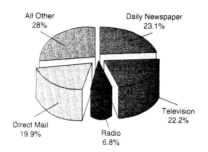

		1992[1] (millions)	% of Total	1993[2] (millions)	% of Total	% of Change
Daily Newspapers	Total	30,639	23.4	31,906	23.1	4.1
	National	3,834	2.9	3,853	2.8	0.5
	Retail	16,041	12.2	16,874	12.2	5.2
	Classified	10,764	8.2	11,179	8.1	3.9
Magazines		7,000	5.3	7,420	5.4	6.0
Television	Total	29,409	22.4	30,600	22.2	4.0
	Network	9,549	7.3	10,435	7.6	9.3
	Spot	15,630	11.9	16,175	11.7	3.5
	Syndication	2,070	1.6	1,480	1.1	-28.5[4]
	Cable	2,160	1.6	2,510	1.8	16.2
Radio		8,654	6.6	9,390	6.8	8.5
Farm Publications		231	0.2	245	0.2	6.1
Direct Mail		25,391	19.4	27,425	19.9	8.0
Business Publications		3,090	2.4	3,200	2.3	3.6
Outdoor		1,031	0.8	1,020	0.7	-1.1
Yellow Pages		9,320	7.1	9,515	6.9	2.1
Miscellaneous		16,427	12.5	17,125	12.4	4.2
Grand Total–National		76,252	58.1	80,473	58.4	5.5
Grand Total–Local[3]		54,940	41.9	57,373	41.6	4.4
TOTAL—ALL MEDIA		131,192	100.0	137,846	100.0	5.1

[1]Revised data; [2]Preliminary estimates; [3]Includes newspaper retail and classified categories; [4]Not comparable with previous years when Fox was included in Syndication. Fox is now included in network.

Source: McCann-Erickson Inc., NAA

115

1. *Flexibility.* The medium offers a wide variety of ways to illustrate a product; copy can be either detailed or condensed; the size of the ad can provide the impact of a full page or can be limited to fractional space to accommodate the budget.
2. *Fast results.* Results are evident almost immediately following an ad's appearance, perhaps within two or three days.
3. *Short lead time.* An ad can be placed very close to the publication date of the paper, giving the advertiser the advantages of last minute changes and fast action on decisions.
4. *Wide coverage.* Circulation is aimed at a compact geographic area, the advertiser's concentrated target market, as a rule.

Most of the retail advertising in daily newspapers is local advertising. Retailers must target their own trading areas in order to draw traffic and avoid wasted circulation, and local papers do that best.

In addition to the daily news sections, most newspapers publish special sections on entertainment and fashion or style and Sunday supplements. The advertiser assesses which of these will produce the best results, generally with the assistance of the newspaper's advertising representative.

There are also many local and regional newspapers that provide good advertising outlets for the retailer, such as local business reviews, shopping guides, newsletters from county arts councils, and small weekly community newspapers, all of which charge lower rates than daily papers.

Once the retailer has earmarked budget dollars for newspaper advertising, additional decisions must be made. The following factors must be considered as the retailer plans the store's newspaper campaign.

Concentration.   The more intensive the use of a medium, the more effective it becomes. Inconsistent use of any medium provides lukewarm results. The retailer must decide how often to run ads in a particular newspaper.

Size. The larger the ad, the greater the impression it makes. But the decision on ad size is reached after taking into account the retailer's budget and the results the ad is intended to produce.

Color. While black-and-white ads are used quite effectively with high-quality photography and art, color increases readership significantly. Issues of reproduction quality and higher costs must be considered when weighing the value of adding color to newspaper ads.

Position. The page and the space that the advertisement occupies in the newspaper is called position. Naturally, the advertiser wants the ad to have the best chance of being noticed. For the highest visibility, the advertiser may choose a *"preferred"* *position,* either in the first few pages of the general news section or in the Fashion or Lifestyle sections where fashion-related news appears. In theory, the preferred position trains the store's customers to look for the store's ad; they become accustomed to seeing the ad in a given spot. As a rule it is more expensive to run an ad in a preferred position. For a lower cost, the advertiser might choose a *run-of-paper* or ROP position. ROP ads are placed anywhere in the paper at the publisher's discretion and are generally the most feasible option for the small retailer.

Newspaper Format.   A newspaper is identified by size either as a *broadsheet*, the standard large size, or a tabloid, which is approximately half the size of a broadsheet. The broadsheet is six columns wide; the *tabloid* is five columns wide. The retailer weighs the store's image and the readership profiles of the papers in deciding which format is appropriate.

The Standard Advertising Unit (SAU) system, shown in Figure 9.3, standardizes the units by which advertising space is purchased. Ads are measured by column width and depth in inches. The more columns and inches the ad spans, the higher the cost. Each newspaper has a printed *rate schedule* that determines what each unit of space will cost. When a retailer plans to run a newspaper ad, an advertising space salesperson will discuss rates and select the size of the ad according to the budget.

Paper Stock.   Newspapers are printed on paper called *newsprint,* an off-white pulpy stock of inexpensive quality. Newsprint comes in different qualities; it may be light or heavy, rough or smooth. The higher-quality newsprint is often chosen for magazine supplements or fashion sections where accurate reproduction is important and when better detail and color are sought.

Timing

When it comes to selling fashion, timing is the lifeblood of the business. In order to maintain its fashion identity, the store must be attuned to the earliest glimmer of a trend and be ready to buy merchandise aggressively and to back its philosophy with dynamic advertising.

To assume fashion leadership in the community, the store needs the ability to turn on a dime. This means that the buyers and fashion directors are constantly in the market and at fashion shows, observing changes in lifestyles, music, and cultural attitudes. They are sensitive to all that affects what we wear and how we wear it, viewing fashion as the end expression of what is happening in the world and our immediate surroundings.

To the advertising director, timing is all of that and more. For an advertising program to produce desired sales, advertising must be timed to the customer's buying patterns.

Comprehensive record-keeping offers valuable insights into sales patterns as they are affected by weather, holidays, and even promotions in other depart-

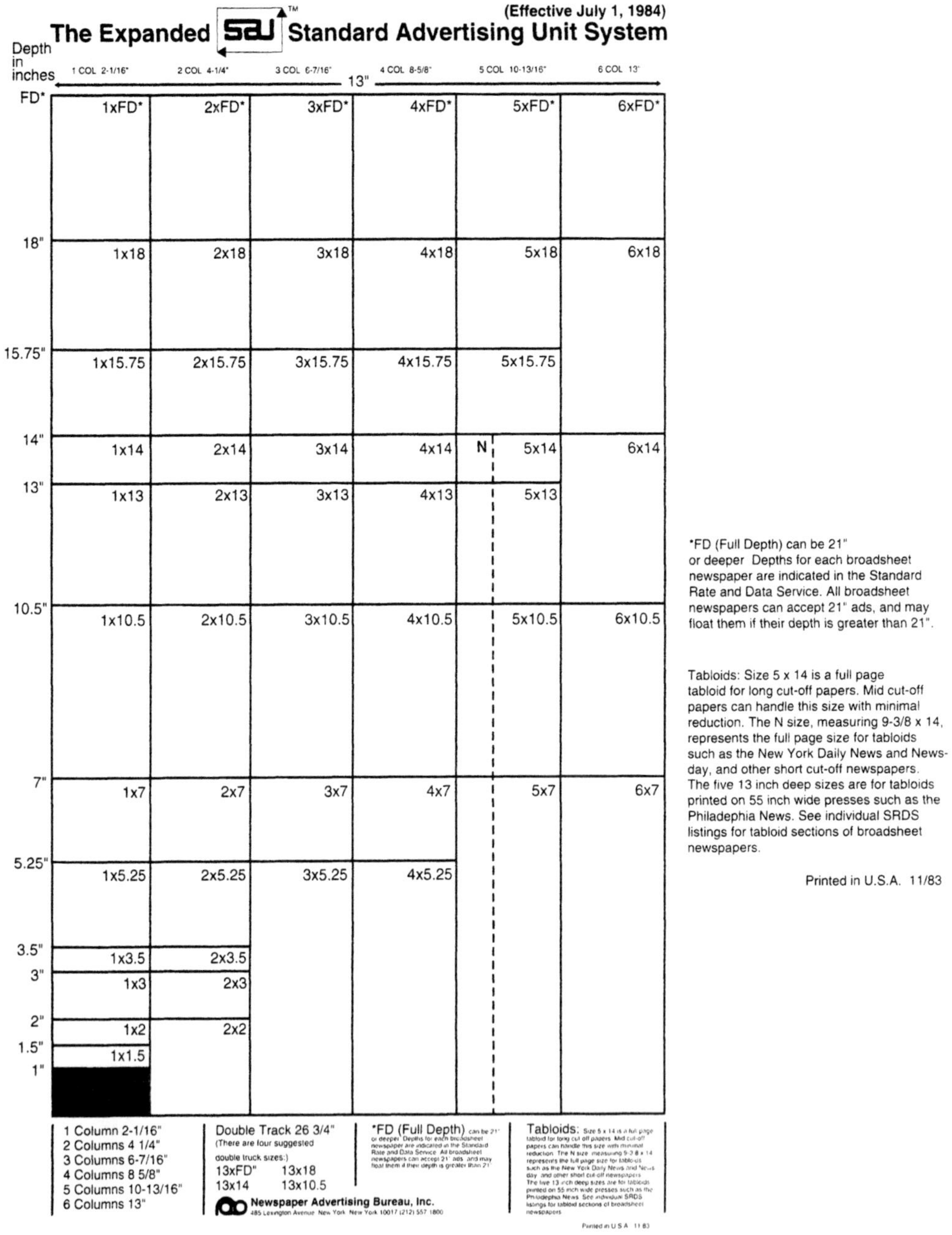

The Expanded SAU™ Standard Advertising Unit System

(Effective July 1, 1984)

Depth in inches

	1 COL 2-1/16"	2 COL 4-1/4"	3 COL 6-7/16"	4 COL 8-5/8"	5 COL 10-13/16"	6 COL 13"
FD*	1xFD*	2xFD*	3xFD*	4xFD*	5xFD*	6xFD*
18"	1x18	2x18	3x18	4x18	5x18	6x18
15.75"	1x15.75	2x15.75	3x15.75	4x15.75	5x15.75	
14"	1x14	2x14	3x14	4x14	5x14	6x14
13"	1x13	2x13	3x13	4x13	5x13	
10.5"	1x10.5	2x10.5	3x10.5	4x10.5	5x10.5	6x10.5
7"	1x7	2x7	3x7	4x7	5x7	6x7
5.25"	1x5.25	2x5.25	3x5.25	4x5.25		
3.5"	1x3.5	2x3.5				
3"	1x3	2x3				
2"	1x2	2x2				
1.5"	1x1.5					
1"						

*FD (Full Depth) can be 21" or deeper. Depths for each broadsheet newspaper are indicated in the Standard Rate and Data Service. All broadsheet newspapers can accept 21" ads, and may float them if their depth is greater than 21".

Tabloids: Size 5 x 14 is a full page tabloid for long cut-off papers. Mid cut-off papers can handle this size with minimal reduction. The N size, measuring 9-3/8 x 14, represents the full page size for tabloids such as the New York Daily News and Newsday, and other short cut-off newspapers. The five 13 inch deep sizes are for tabloids printed on 55 inch wide presses such as the Philadelphia News. See individual SRDS listings for tabloid sections of broadsheet newspapers.

Printed in U.S.A. 11/83

1 Column 2-1/16"
2 Columns 4 1/4"
3 Columns 6-7/16"
4 Columns 8 5/8"
5 Columns 10-13/16"
6 Columns 13"

Double Track 26 3/4"
(There are four suggested double truck sizes:)
13xFD"   13x18
13x14   13x10.5

Newspaper Advertising Bureau, Inc.
485 Lexington Avenue New York New York 10017 (212) 557 1800

Figure 9.3

Standard newspaper sizes are called tabloid (five columns wide) and broadsheet (six columns wide). A Standard Advertising Unit system is used to measure space. Copyright Newspaper Advertising Bureau, Inc.

ments. Statistical studies of monthly retail sales by category and household are other useful indexes for the timing of advertising.

As we have already discussed, advertising is planned to coincide with the normal fluctuations in a classification of business. It is the most cost-effective way to spend the advertising budget.

Cost of Space

The store's first concern in advertising is to create an ad that will produce volume increases proportionate to the money invested in the ad. Retailers look for returns in percentages.

A sale ad, for example, is expected to produce a return in sales of roughly ten times. In dollars, if an ad investment of $10,000 is made, the store expects $100,000 in resulting sales.

In the case of fashion ads, the guidelines are somewhat different. The investment in a newsprint fashion ad is based on the investment made in merchandise rather than space. Therefore, a small dollar investment in merchandise requires a lesser advertising expenditure; that is, the retailer would run a small ad. The larger the investment in merchandise, the larger the need to generate sales and, thus, a larger ad.

Rates for newspaper ads are determined by size, position in the newspaper, and the frequency with which the advertiser runs ads in the paper. Local papers offer various inducements in the form of volume rates, meaning the more space purchased, the lower the cost per inch or line.

To be assured space and preferential positions, retailers who can afford to project their budgets sign yearly contracts with newspapers.

Preparing the Ad

As discussed in Chapter 8, the buyer provides the advertising department with an information sheet listing all the salient details about the fashions that are to be advertised. This information is distributed to the copy chief and art director, who then meet to discuss the best approach for the ad.

Rough sketches are made; ideas are presented and exchanged on how layout, copy, and artwork should look. The concept grows and evolves. During this phase, many revisions are made, ideas are abandoned. When there is a meeting of minds, preliminary copy and sketches are combined in a rough layout to give a visual idea of how the ad will look in its final form, with headline, text, and illustration or photo suggested.

Following approval of the rough, the art department begins work on the finished ad.

During this time, the copywriter is polishing the ad copy under the supervision of the copy chief. The buyer or fashion director keeps close tabs on the work in progress to see that ideas are taking shape as planned and discussed. Proofs are checked for correct spelling, proper manufacturer attribution, and prices.

When the ad is finalized it moves into the hands of the production manager, whose job it is to complete and deliver it "press ready" to the newspapers in which it will appear.

ELEMENTS OF A PRINTED AD

As the newsprint ad is put into work, each of its parts—copy, artwork, and layout plan—evolves into a unit.

Copy. "Copy" refers to the words used to sell in an advertisement. In broadcast advertising, these words are first written, then spoken. In newsprint advertising, they are read and thus seen as an integral part of the visual structure of the ad. With this dual function in mind, the copywriter considers how the shape of the text will integrate with the artwork while composing a compelling sales pitch.

While basic tenets hold for all advertising copy, retail ad copy is a slightly different breed. It must speak the language of fashion, understand the underlying psychology of selling, and provide very basic information (price, color, sizes, and so on) with a degree of finesse, all in keeping with store image. The content of the copy is ultimately the product of a mind trained in transporting the verbal into the visual...and back again, using information provided by the store's buyers.

There are cases, such as in Figure 9.4, when the copy is the dominant element of an ad. This kind of ad is well suited to institutional advertising and must rely on attractive typography and layout to attract and hold the reader's attention. The copy itself must be interesting, arresting, and polished.

Copy elements are divided into visible components that help to highlight the message and relieve the monotony of solid copy blocks.

> *Headlines* are foremost elements. Usually set in the largest-size type, headlines are written to intrigue the reader and draw his or her interest to the ad. They can consist of a banner slogan, a designer's name, or a single word with maximum impact.
>
> *Subheadlines* may or may not be used. These are generally set in smaller type than the headline in order not to compete with the headline. Subheads are used when the headline needs explanation or expanding.
>
> *Body copy* is the text which contains the "sell" of the ad. It may include detailed information about the items featured or merely state price, sizes, or fabrics.
>
> *Logo*, or logotype, is the name of the store created as a graphic design. It is most important for this highly identifiable symbol to appear in all advertising to provide an indelible connection with the store in the reader's mind.

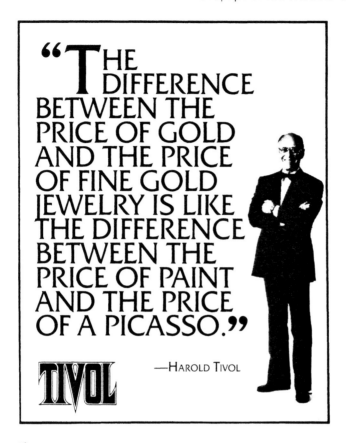

Figure 9.4

What makes this institutional advertisement striking is the large copy block which dominates most of the ad's space. Copyright Newspaper Advertising Bureau, Inc.

Artwork.   As there are extremes in the presentation of ad copy, so there are extremes in the all-important art which is the ad's basic underpinning.

By art, we refer to the visuals, or the illustration or photograph of the merchandise for sale. In retail fashion advertising, the art expresses the fashion prominence of the item shown. It is glamorized by the model wearing it and accessorized or put together as current fashion dictates.

Fashion illustrators' renderings can be equally as effective as photography, and many a store has established its identity with the consistent use of an artist's distinct style of brushwork. For example, before his rise to historical fame as a leader of the Pop Art movement, Andy Warhol illustrated footwear for I. Miller.

Layout.   In the art department, a layout artist sketches one or more rough outlines of the way the advertisement will look, based on the copy elements that are to be used (heads, subheads, and body copy) and artwork.

Although the first layout is considered rough, it begins to project the energy of the final product. Revisions will be made on the rough layout until it is finally approved by the art director and the buyer. In the next step, the comprehensive layout or "comp" is made. At this stage, all the copy and art are in place, exactly as they will appear in the printed ad, except that the artwork may be simulated in a felt-tipped pen sketch to resemble the final photograph or illustration.

At this point, a go-ahead is given on the final artwork. If it is to be photographed, the photographer selects the models and locations; the fashion director and buyer collect the merchandise. Hairstylists and makeup artists go into action on the set, preparing the models for the camera. A photostylist dresses the models and accessorizes their costumes. Following the photo session or "shoot," the photographer submits proofs to the art director, who will in turn select the best shots. From the "selects," the art department chooses the one shot that will be used.

If the ad is to be illustrated, the artist completes the final artwork, which is then subject to approval or revision by the art director.

Production.   Following approval of the comprehensive layout, the final stage begins. The final layout, copy, and artwork are sent to the production department, where the production manager proceeds to pull all the components of the ad together.

Production orders the copy to be set in print according to typeface specifications (size and style) which are selected. Artwork is reproduced into high-quality prints, and the final layout is set in place, or pasted up.

After it is once again approved, production sends the finished mechanical and proofs to the newspaper. The newspaper takes a picture of the mechanical and uses this negative to print the ad.

Summary

Newspaper advertising remains the medium most used by fashion retailers. Despite increased advertising activity in the electronic media, local daily papers receive the bulk of retail advertising.

Newspapers boast an audience that is better educated and are found in upper-income households, the target customer for most fashion retailers. Additionally, newspapers as an advertising medium offer flexibility, fast results, short lead time for the preparation of the ad, and coverage which reaches the store's target market effectively and cost efficiently.

Preparation of newsprint ads requires a team effort by advertising professionals, the buyer, and the fashion director. The successful newspaper campaign takes into consideration factors of concentration, size of ads, and whether a preferred position in the paper is warranted.

Terms for Review

1. Preferred position
2. Run-of-paper
3. Broadsheet
4. Tabloid
5. Rate schedule
6. Newsprint

Study Review Questions

1. What would you say is the reason that newspaper advertising is regarded as having the authority associated with the press?
2. Besides lower cost, what other advantages does newspaper advertising afford the retailer?
3. Why is concentration a consideration when planning the store's newspaper campaign?
4. What is taken into account when determining the size of a newspaper ad?
5. Why would a store pay more for a preferred position?
6. What does run-of-paper mean?
7. Why is timing important for retail advertising?
8. What affects the rate a retailer pays for newspaper advertising?

Case

You are the advertising director of the Anyplace Department Store. You work with all the buyers of the various departments and with the merchandise managers in planning the store's advertising campaign. In a conference with you, the buyer for the men's department expresses a desire to put half of the budget into television advertising in order to add "zing" to the advertising campaign. The menswear buyer contends that the color and excitement of men's accessories and sportswear could be better conveyed on TV. The buyer also points out that the trend in fashion advertising is moving toward TV, and as the fashion leader in the area, Anyplace Department Store should make the leap into TV advertising.

The store has been using two daily papers in the city and has viewed the newspapers' readership as a close match with the store's target customer. The only area TV station is in the next city.

Questions

1. Explain why some of the advertising dollars spent on a TV commercial would be wasted.

2. How could you answer the buyer's desire to show color but still use newspaper advertising?

3. If you decided to "test" a TV ad, what kind of information would you request from the buyer after the ad appears?

10 BROADCAST ADVERTISING: Radio

Radio has a ubiquitous quality about it. In part, this is due to the kind of companionship radio provides. It is less demanding than the other media; it doesn't require our undivided attention. Instead, it comes along and accompanies us whether we are sautéing in the kitchen or browning at the beach. It runs with us on a jog or rides with us in the car. It wakes us in the morning or soothes us to sleep at night.

Radio programming offers choices to match our mood, our age, our varied tastes. From news to a wide variety of music, from opinions and talk to sports games and analysis, the radio has something for us all.

Radio and the Retail Advertiser

There is an immediacy about radio, a sense that it is timely and current. This can be an advantage to the radio advertiser, especially the fashion retailer. Radio also has the distinct advantage of focusing very sharply on a given target market. Facts and figures describing listeners are collected in surveys made by audience research services. The Radio Advertising Bureau (RAB), a national sales organization serving the radio industry, collects and disseminates these facts about radio listeners to radio stations, which in turn, makes them available to advertisers. The retailer can match its target customer with this demographic information and utilize radio as a vehicle to reach the intended audience.

Few retailers use radio exclusively for their advertising efforts. Instead, radio supplies the retailer with an additional outlet for the sales promotion message. In this chapter, we will examine how radio fits into the communication puzzle, its advantages and disadvantages, and how the fashion retailer utilizes it.

ADVANTAGES OF RADIO

We have already identified radio as a medium of immediacy. A primary appeal of radio advertising is its here-and-now quality.

Timing is an important facet of radio advertising for the fashion retailer. The topic of timing includes not only when the ad will reach the intended listener, but also ad production considerations.

Consider the demographics we said each station has available to the perspective advertiser. The sales representative from a local radio station can identify not only who comprises the listening audience, but when the target audience is listening. Figure 10.1, for example, identifies who listens to the radio during the hours of 7:00 P.M. to midnight, broken down by age, sex, and location while "tuning in." This type of demographic information helps the retailer zero in on the audience it is attempting to reach. The statistics in Figure 10.1 are general; the local station representative would have information that breaks the listening audience down further.

From the available data, the retailer can select a station which best serves the store's needs. As is true with any advertising, the prime objective is to get the best return on investment. And, as is true with all sales promotion efforts, the retailer

Radio Reaches 7 Out Of 10
In Tv's Prime Time

Evening Radio Listeners Average
Almost 5½ Hours A Week

	Evening Reach (Mon. - Sun., 7 PM-Mid.)	Weekly Time Spent Among Listeners
Persons 12 +	71.0%	5:22
Teens 12-17	89.6	6:27
Men		
18+	71.5%	5:17
18-34	84.1	5:44
25-54	75.0	4:58
Women		
18+	65.8%	5:05
18-34	79.3	3:58
25-54	69.0	4:46

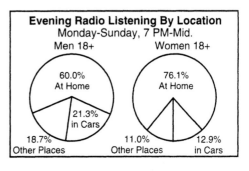

Evening Radio Listening By Location
Monday-Sunday, 7 PM-Mid.

Men 18+   Women 18+

Figure 10.1

Demographic statistics and charts like these are used to "sell" the retailer on the value of radio time. Courtesy of Radio Advertising Bureau.

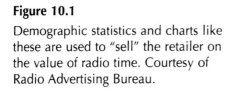

must make sure that the message conveys the intended store image tailored to the store's target customer. Otherwise, the message will not reach the intended audience.

The timing factor also includes production and scheduling considerations. While it is true that most retail advertising is planned long in advance, there are instances that require fast action on the part of the retailer—an end-of-season promotional item offered to a buyer, an unexpected change in the weather, or an event which provides the retailer with an unexpected opportunity. In such cases, radio is a convenient choice. A *radio spot* can be quickly produced and scheduled shortly before airing, making the radio ad far more flexible than newsprint, which requires more steps in the production of the ad.

Radio advertising is relatively inexpensive, when the ability to select the audience and the reach of the medium is considered.

Radio provides intimacy to the retailer's message. A human voice can be persuasive; radio enables the store to send its message one to one, speaker to listener.

The radio spot provides the retailer with flexibility and versatility. The radio ad can be institutional or promotional in nature, hard sell and aggressive, or soft sell and image building. The choice of the speaker, as much as the content of the ad, affects what the listener hears and how he or she reacts. A sales ad, for instance, read by an authoritative voice in a hurried manner is intended to prompt immediate action by the listener. Conversely, through choice of background music and the speaker's voice, the radio spot can communicate the store's personality and character; the audio adds a dimension not available in the print media.

Humor is often effective in advertising, and radio enables the retailer to use this tool. Humor is also used in the other advertising vehicles, but since timing and voice intonation are so crucial to delivery, radio provides a level of control not available in the print ad.

Figure 10.2 is an example of a humorous radio spot. It is also an example of another advantage radio provides the retailer—support for a major sales promotion campaign. Retailers often use radio to add to the message that is being sent through other advertising vehicles. In this case, Maas Brothers uses humor to get across information about the week-long special event in the store and to support the newspaper ad also shown in Figure 10.2.

The theory behind the practice is that one medium reinforces the message in the other, and thus more effectively drives the message home. For example, one prospective customer may have read about the event and is "reminded" by the radio spot. Another may first hear about California Spirit on the radio and further investigate it when reading the newspaper. Additionally, using more than one medium increases the reach of the message and enables the retailer to communicate with a wider audience.

DISADVANTAGES OF RADIO

The biggest disadvantage of radio advertising is that it is aired and lost. It cannot be clipped and saved; it is not retrievable. This disadvantage is countered by

WORD ASSOCIATION

Tick-tock of clock in background

DR: Okay, Miss Haberdunk, we're going to try a little word association...

SHE: Alrighty, Doctor.

DR: I'll say a word and you say the first thing that comes to mind. Ready?

SHE: Uh-huh.

DR: Sourdough bread.

SHE: Maas Brothers.

DR: Eva Gabor.

SHE: Maas Brothers.

DR: Trolley cars.

SHE: Maas Brothers.

DR: Miss Haberdunk, all the things I mentioned are in California, why do you keep saying...

SHE: Well, California is now in Florida, Doctor. At Maas Brothers.

DR: I think you're loony-tunes, Miss Haberdunk.

SHE: No, California is in Florida from March 1st throught March 8th during Maas Brothers California Spirit Excitement. Eva Gabor will be there...

DR: Really?

SHE: Sure, and you can win a trip to California via United Airlines and stay at Hyatt Hotels, or maybe win a Hobie Cat Sailboat...and there's no purchase necessary.

DR: All at Maas Brothers?

SHE: At Westshore, Tyrone, Countryside, Sarasota Uptown

DR: Maas Brothers, March 1st through March 8th... (CUCKOO, CUCKOO)

SHE: Oh, you have a cuckoo clock.

DR: No, that's my next patient.

ANNCR: Visit California right here in Florida at Maas Brothers, of course.

Figure 10.2

This radio spot used humor to send a message about a Maas Brothers' promotion. The radio spot reinforces the newspaper ad about the event. Courtesy of *Retail Ad Week* magazine.

repeating the ad—thereby increasing the chance that the ad is heard by the intended audience and that its message is retained.

Radio cannot offer a visual image other than through words and sounds. This drawback prevents the fashion retailer from introducing a new fashion silhouette or presenting the subtlety of this season's colors.

While demographic profiles help the retailer to purchase air time when its target customer has the radio on, there is no guarantee that the target customer is "tuned in." We have already identified radio as a companion medium; the other activity could distract the listener just as the radio spot airs. Similarly, the listener may simply not pay attention to the retailer's message amid the clutter of advertising messages aired on the radio.

The Radio Spot

The radio commercial starts with a written script. The script includes the copy of the commercial—the words that will be spoken—and instructions for any background sounds such as music, sound effects, and so on. If the commercial will include more than one speaker, the script clearly indicates who says what and when.

The script could be delivered by professional actors, the radio program host, or a representative from the store. It has become increasingly popular of late for a company president to act as spokesperson, but this option should be pursued with caution; a person's business expertise is oftentimes not equaled by an ability to effectively deliver a selling message.

The commercial can be read live on air or recorded on a master tape. The latter option allows for more control over the resulting ad and is the more logical choice when background music or sound effects are used.

Sound must create selling appeal nonvisually. In order to activate the listener's imagination, good radio commercials create powerful visual imagery, thought pictures that prod our emotions and trigger a response—in this case, to go to the store and buy its products. This must occur within the limits of the length of the commercial spot: 10, 30, or 60 seconds.

Since the customer is hearing rather than reading the advertisement, memory retention is somewhat hindered. The commercial, brief and transient, intrudes unexpectedly during the program, usually while the listener is thinking about or doing other things. By the time the ad has caught the listener's interest, much of the essential information the advertiser hopes to convey has passed by. For this reason, radio ads are repeated at well-chosen intervals during the day. Repetition serves not only to impress the selling points of the commercial on the same listener, but increases the number of potential customers hearing the ad.

During the course of the commercial, the store's name is usually mentioned more than once to be certain the listener registers the name of the sponsor. Most advertisers prefer mention of the store name at least three times, and possibly more, during the spot.

The words read aloud in a radio commercial are written very differently from those in printed ads. Although radio ads are often created to support newsprint advertising, the radio script is not simply converted bits of newspaper ad copy.

Radio copy is most successful when it is written in a warm, personal style; the listener should feel that the message is directed at him or her alone.

The radio scriptwriter attempts at the start of the commercial to break through the listener's resistance. Attention-getting phrases or sound effects are the radio commercial's headline. The aim is to attract the listener's attention and let the listener know that the message that will follow is intended for that individual's ears. To accomplish this, the scriptwriter must "know" the target of the ad; only a thorough understanding of the target customer's needs, desires, and lifestyle will enable the scriptwriter to successfully capture the listener's attention.

In the seconds that follow, and in as few words as possible, the store or product is sold. The emphasis in the copy must be on customer benefits. Like all good ad copy, radio copy is concise, composed of simple, direct phases that get to the point quickly. Simplicity is imperative; the radio commercial jammed with too many facts about too many products only confuses the listener.

The store name and major selling points should be repeated during the ad—but only up to a point. When it becomes an obvious ploy, repetition can be irritating, creating a negative impression.

Almost any item or idea can be successfully promoted in a radio commercial, provided the ad can create a mental picture for the listener. Choosing items with broad rather than limited appeal is a rule of thumb for radio advertising. Since the listener must be able to quickly grasp what is being offered, specific fashion items ads are considered less suitable for radio ads than thematic approaches or special promotions. For example, a commercial announcing a back-to-school sale with selected classifications and prices cited has a better chance at creating the desired mental picture and obtaining the desired result—sales—than an ad focusing on the newest fashion look.

As we identified before, radio commercials often are used to back up newspaper ads for special store events as in Figure 10.2; it makes more sense to give detailed information in a form that can be clipped and carried than to fill 30 seconds with more information than the listener can possibly absorb. Instead, the radio ad talks about the event in general terms or concentrates on a few topics to create interest. In the case of the Maas Brothers radio spot, these "high notes" included Eva Gabor, win a trip, win a sailboat. The vehicle to deliver these high notes was a conversation between a psychologist and his patient; the tone of the ad was humorous. But note that not one mention was made of the real reason for the special event, that is, to sell merchandise.

Do not confuse this general focus with generalizations; to be effective the radio ad must be pared down, not watered down.

Buying Radio Time

We have looked at some of the advantages radio spot advertising offers the fashion retailer and some of the drawbacks of the medium. As with all sales promotion activities, the retailer must consider the store's customer and the store's image. The decision to buy air time would include the following considerations:

- The station's programming policy—does it match the store's image?
- The station's audience profile—who listens to the station; how many people does the station reach?
- Who else advertises with the station?
- Is this the appropriate medium to carry the message to the target customer?

When a store plans a straight institutional campaign, it may elect to do so in order to promote a new or changing policy, to boost its public image, or simply to remind its customer where it stands in terms of fashion focus and customer services.

A service commercial explains what the store offers to the customer to make shopping there convenient and attractive, focusing on such topics as free shopping services, restaurants, free delivery, ample parking, or a liberal return policy.

Of course, as with print advertising, an institutional message is often woven into an item or event radio spot by inserting a phrase or two into the end or beginning of a 30- or 60-second spot.

Because of its immediacy, the radio commercial can be used to convey late-breaking information to the customer. According to the Radio Advertising Bureau, [radio spots] "are especially useful when merchandise is delayed in reaching the store, or a schedule on radio has been so successful that the store is out of stock."

Air time for broadcast media is best purchased by an individual experienced in media buying. Large stores that buy a lot of radio time have an in-house specialist. There are also media-buying services that can be hired to represent both the large and small retailer. Finally, many stations have media representatives who are available to work with the retailer.

Radio offers spots in 10-, 30-, or 60-second lengths; the most popular spot length is 30 seconds.

The budget appropriation earmarked for radio advertising is usually determined at the start of the planning year. This budget decision must take into account what is needed to create a radio campaign substantial enough to achieve the store's goals combined with how much the store is able to afford.

Based on promotional and institutional objectives set by the store, the radio budget is apportioned to cover merchandise classifications, divisions, and departments, usually within a six-month plan.

SELECTING THE STATION

Listener demographics and psychographics, distributed by such marketing organizations as the RAB, are selling tools used by stations in marketing their time and services. Based on these surveys, broadcasters can estimate which programs will reach the store's target audience.

The advertiser selects a station by the kind of audience it can deliver. When there are a number of competing stations in a local area from which to choose, the store can become more selective, looking for the best rate deals and considering programming and the caliber of the station's other local and national advertisers.

Radio frequency is another consideration when purchasing radio time. *AM frequency* radio stations broadcast over a broader geographical area, but *FM frequency* stations offer static-free, superior sound reproduction. The retailer must weigh the quality factor against the station's audience profiles to determine which frequency best reaches the store's audience.

HOW MUCH TIME?

When the proper station has been selected, the media buyer will place an order for a time schedule during which the commercials will run. The number and length of radio spots will determine the depth of saturation of the campaign.

A decision is made as to what percentage of the market will be exposed to the message each week, measured by *reach* (how many different people hear the commercial at least once in a given time period) and *frequency* (the average number of times an individual listener hears the commercial).

To determine audience exposure, reach is multiplied by frequency. From this information, the station representative and the media buyer decide how many spots a day are needed to cover the desired target audience.

For higher reach, a retailer will buy spots on many stations; to get higher frequency, it will buy on fewer stations and increase the number of times the ad is run.

Retail advertisers try to strike a balance between frequency and reach, and many stations can now provide them with computerized estimates to aid in scheduling their commercials.

RATE STRUCTURES

The station provides the advertiser with a rate card which breaks down the cost of air time by parts of the day, the length of the commercial, and how many times it will run.

The advertiser can buy on a weekly or yearly plan. The station may provide cost-saving plans and services as inducements.

Rates are naturally higher for the times of day that are in most demand; these are graded by letters—AA, A, B, C, and D. The highest cost would be for Class AA and the lowest for Class D. Stations vary, and so do their rates, but the following is a typical way of classifying air time:

Class AA:	Morning Drive Time—6 A.M.–10 A.M.
Class B:	Home Worker Time—10 A.M.–4 P.M.
Class A:	Evening Drive Time—4 P.M.–7 P.M.
Class C:	Evening Time—7 P.M.–midnight
Class D:	Night Time—midnight–6 A.M.

Summary

Radio as an advertising medium offers the retailer the advantage of its immediacy in reaching and eliciting response from its potential customers, and in reaching a sharply defined target audience.

Most retail radio advertising occurs at the local level where listeners are close to the retail outlet.

Within the period of a radio commercial, an item, event, or service may be advertised, or a combination of two or more of these. Radio is regarded by many retail advertisers as support advertising for other advertising efforts and as the medium of choice for conveying late-breaking information to the retailer's target audience.

The chain of events in the production of a scheduled radio commercial is as follows: (1) the advertising and sales promotion departments determine the total media budget, a portion of which is allocated to radio; (2) the media buyer selects a radio station or stations and purchases time; (3) the scriptwriter creates a script indicating dialogue, music, sound effects; (4) the producer pulls all the elements together, using actors, musicians, sound technicians, and so on; (5) a master tape is cut, approved, and reproduced; (6) the commercial is aired.

The cost of the radio spot is determined by the time of day it runs and the size of the audience it reaches. The larger the audience and the more desirable the program on which it runs, the higher the cost.

Terms for Review

1. Radio spot
2. AM frequency
3. FM frequency
4. Reach
5. Frequency

Study Review Questions

1. What are the advantages of radio advertising?
2. What are the disadvantages of radio advertising?
3. Repetition is the key to memory retention. What implication does this statement have for radio advertising?
4. What is the advantage of repeating an ad on the radio?
5. In a radio commercial for a store, how frequently should the store's name be given? Why?
6. What is meant by *reach* and *frequency* in radio broadcasting?
7. What is the overriding consideration when a retailer is considering using radio as an advertising medium?

Case

The following is a first draft of a 30-second radio spot for Anyplace Department Store.

Warehouse Savings

Ed: My name is Ed and I'm a security guard. For weeks now I've been watching over all the merchandise Anyplace Department Store has put together for their big two-day warehouse sale. It's going to happen Saturday and Sunday only. Take it from me, this sale is big. Over a million dollars' worth of merchandise, at fantastic low sale prices. You want some proof, listen to this.

Announcer: Comforters in full, queen, and king sizes for $10.95. Mattress pads and bed sacks in twin and full sizes, $6.95. Also, washers and dryers, microwave ovens, and sofas—all at unbeatable prices.

Ed: D'ya hear that? You can't find better prices, but you'd better hurry. I notice some brands are limited. So I'll see you there. Tell them Ed, the security guard, sent you.

Announcer: Anyplace's two-day warehouse sale. Saturday eight to five and Sunday ten to five, at 225 Main Street. Free round-trip shuttle bus service from Anyplace's downtown. Anyplace's two-day warehouse sale, Saturday and Sunday only.

Questions

1. What background sound effects would you add to the script?
2. What do you think is more important for an ad like this—reach or frequency?
3. Do you think the ad would attract customers to the sale? What improvements would you add to the script?

11 BROADCAST ADVERTISING: Television

Television is so much an integral part of our lives that existence without it is almost inconceivable. We tend to take for granted this powerful and pervasive influence reaching into our homes, and, with the advances that made TV portable, any place we choose to cart it.

All media rely on stimulating the senses to get an ad's message across; radio relies on sound, the print media on sight. TV, however, communicates through sound, color, and motion in a combination that attracts and holds the viewer's attention. While it can be argued that CD-ROM offers the same elements, the omnipresent television is a powerful medium indeed.

Long regarded as an impressive advertising tool, TV's role has been further strengthened by the rapid growth of cable. According to the Cabletelevision Advertising Bureau, cable penetration has expanded to two-thirds of all American households and is projected to climb to 72% by the year 2000.

Cable has become part of our national culture. Cable channels such as CNN and Nickelodeon are as recognizable as any national network. More important, cable has had a profound effect on fashion sales promotion, especially for the small retailer.

While broadcast TV traditionally had been too expensive and far reaching for most small businesses, cable TV, with its low rates, affordable production, and targeted viewership, quickly became a viable and effective facet of the small retailer's total sales promotion effort. The Cabletelevision Advertising Bureau reports that the total cable advertising revenues of $4.4 billion in 1994 represents a 359% increase since 1986.

Other developments altering the landscape include infomercials, TV home-shopping channels, and technology that will enable the TV viewer to interact with the television.

As a television format, *infomercials* appear to be regular programming but are really paid commercials extending over 30 or sometimes 60 minutes. Infomercials and home-shopping channels represent a nonstore form of selling. The increased popularity of both has prompted speculation that major retailers will some day be forced to offer merchandise through these avenues to remain profitable. In fact, Macy's flirted with the concept in 1993.

In both the case of the infomercials and the home-shopping channels, television acts as a display case for the merchandise. To close the sale, the viewer must go to the phone and order the merchandise. However, the technology is already in place to enable the customer to interact with the commercial, thus dramatically changing television's role in the world of fashion retailing.

In this world of "virtual reality," the television would not only display the merchandise, but take the customer's order as well. The customer would be able to order merchandise custom-made by using a keypad to enter personal measurements for the garment offered. Some predict that by the year 2000 up to one-half of all the homes in the United States will be physically capable of receiving interactive television.

Even those excited about the prospect of interactive television identify two major obstacles. The first concerns the hefty cost of wiring homes with coaxial or fiber-optic cables to enable the two-way communication to take place. The other has to do with customer acceptance. It is argued that TV will be hard-pressed to replace the drama, excitement, and sense of community many find in the retail shopping experience.

The Retailer and TV

Television advertising, as with all aspects of sales promotion, has to be evaluated within the context of the retailer's goals, budget, and the store's target customer.

Retailers have successfully deployed the power of the medium for a variety of reasons, from major campaigns to change their image, to concentrated efforts to generate traffic for a special sale.

The elements of the image, motion, and sound make television a powerful selling tool for the fashion retailer. With its ability to project theme and mood while delivering entertainment and information, the TV ad is a vehicle through which the essence of personality—not only of the merchandise, but of the store itself—can be presented.

The ability to edit and control what the perspective customer sees, hears, and even feels makes television advertising a powerful weapon in the retailer's sales promotion arsenal.

ADVANTAGES OF TELEVISION

Television reaches a large audience and, in some cases, may be more effective in reaching the store's target customer, teenagers for instance, than the other media.

As with radio, television stations are able to provide demographic information on the viewing audience so that the message can be targeted to the store's customers.

While retailing giants have long been able to justify the cost of network television advertising due to the geographic spread of their stores, and large retailers could justify the shotgun coverage of local advertising on station affiliates, local cable has supplied the small retailer with the ability to precisely target geographic zones.

The TV ad is versatile and flexible, both in the message it can convey and in its technical capabilities. It can comprise stills, action, or a combination. It can be general and institutional in nature, or specific and promotional. It can be used to convey a fashion trend, demonstrate selling points, and educate viewers about the merchandise featured.

Through the technical aspects of camera position, editing techniques, voice overs, and the ability to superimpose type, the TV ad can be reworked, reused, and refocused.

The television ad enables the retailer to deliver a message simultaneously to the viewer's sense of sight and sound, thereby increasing the impact of the message and the chances of response.

Finally, manufacturers encourage retailers to use TV as an advertising vehicle by offering co-op money for TV advertising. Many large manufacturers offer ready-made commercials to the retailer, who only has to slot in the store name and pay for the air time.

DISADVANTAGES OF TELEVISION

As with radio, the television ad is aired and then is gone. So, the lack of retrievability is a drawback of television advertising. This factor has been somewhat countered by the practice of programming the VCR to tape a program for later viewing or reviewing, but in general, an interested viewer does not have the ability to go back to and refer to the ad as is the case in the print media.

Cost is another disadvantage. For the message to effectively reach the intended audience, the same principles of reach and frequency discussed in the last chapter hold true for television. While both production and air time costs have been drastically reduced by the local cable option, both still are significant when the retailer is utilizing network or local affiliate air time.

Cost is also a factor in execution. Skilled experts are required if the identified advantages of television advertising are to be realized. The cost of talent, from actors to technicians, from conceptualizers to executers, is expensive.

The time required to prepare the television ad is substantial, especially one which utilizes actors, background music, different angle shots, and sophisticated editing techniques. Obviously, a *static ad,* which combines a photo and text similar to a print ad and are common on local cable, requires much less production time. In general, retailers have to budget for three to four weeks of production time before the television ad is ready for broadcast.

Another disadvantage of television advertising is the limited amount of time available. Clearly, the best time to run an ad is during *prime time*, when the largest audience is watching. But slots for prime time are often purchased by large advertisers at the network level, and even when there is availability, it is costly, a function of supply and demand.

Finally, the fashion retailer has no guarantee that the ad will in fact be viewed by the target customer. Commercials have long been the designated time for the viewer to run out of the room; with the proliferation of remote controls, commercials now act as the green light the newest national pastime. Although there are no concrete research studies, it is logical to assume that many well-produced and thought-out television ads have been done in by "channel surfing."

Planning and Executing the TV Campaign

An advertiser may buy time on either *network* or *local broadcasts*, depending on the audience desired. A network ad is broadcast to several hundred affiliate stations across the country, reaching all but the most remote backwoods communities. Network advertising, as one might expect, is the most expensive choice.

Local station broadcasts are concentrated within a given region. Local time costs are, of course, lower.

Advertisers may choose between two main ad classifications: sponsorship and spot ads. Sponsorship requires a larger dollar investment, but affords the advertiser greater impact and control. As the sole advertiser throughout the length of the program, the sponsor is assured that no other advertising message will conflict with its own. Spot advertising is a less expensive way to reach the target market. A short advertising segment, the spot ad is anywhere from 10 to 60 seconds long, with 30 seconds being the most common spot-ad length.

Cable offers a variety of advertising formats from text-only classifieds to 30-second spots to extended infomercials.

Planning is the first and most crucial step of an advertising campaign. The percentage of the ad budget allocated to TV will depend on the size of the media budget and the needs and expectations of the individual store.

Advertisers generally plan TV campaigns six months in advance. During the planning stage, activities occur in several store divisions simultaneously.

1. *Time is bought.* The media planner must make the time buys well in advance. TV time is a perishable commodity; station salespeople sell it as they would merchandise. The earlier the buy, the better the selection available to the advertiser.

2. *The ad campaign is finalized.* Plans need the approval of management all along the store's chain of command. The overall goal of the ad, and how it will be reached, must be agreed upon.

3. *Co-op advertising support is sought.* The buyers whose classifications or departments are to be featured confirm cooperative support with manufac-

Chorus:

Everyone has different styles, something new to say.
It might be simple, might be chic, or the tailored casual way.
It might look sporty, fancy free, or different from the rest.
But whatever look you've got, it's got to be the best.

So you shop at Saks Fifth Avenue, 'cause your choices all are better
And you like the friendly, helpful people who really seem to care.

We are all the things you are. All the looks of you
We are all the things you are, At Saks Fifth Avenue.

We are all the things you are. All the looks of you
We are all the things you are, At Saks Fifth Avenue.

Figure 11.1

This is a four-frame storyboard of a finished commercial by Saks Fifth Avenue. Through
both the visual elements of the ad and the text, which was set to music, the ad is designed
to reach a variety of target customers and position the store as having something for everyone. Courtesy of the Television Bureau of Advertising.

turers. At the same time, buyers must make certain that the items to be advertised will be delivered and on the floor in time.

4. *Production responsibility is decided.* Only large retailers have in-house TV production people. Most retailers hire outside resources. A good advertising agency can save time, money, and wasted effort. In addition, both local affiliate stations and local cable providers have production services available to the advertiser.

SELECTING THE STATION

Time is to the TV station as inventory is to the retailer. There is desirable and less desirable time in a station's inventory, and it is up to the station's account executive to market that time. The station's rates are based on time periods (day parts) and the size of the audience delivered. Rates may also be based on the extent of competition from other stations (if there are other stations within a given market), the size of the station's inventory of time, and the station's own revenue requirements.

Prior to buying time, the media planner or agency will consider the factors of duplication, or how many times the commercial will reach the same audience; reach, or the percentage of audience exposed to one or more announcements; and frequency, or the average number of times an audience views a TV schedule. Duplication, reach, and frequency vary from one market to the next. The same data is used in buying radio time.

When buying time, a media planner must establish a goal of how many households the store's message is to reach in order to make the commercial cost effective.

The accepted measure for comparison in the broadcast media is the *cost per thousand* (CPM). It is an aid in determining the value received from the spot commercial time. To reach the CPM value, the cost of the air time times 1,000 is divided by the number of households the ad will potentially reach.

$$CPM = \text{cost of commercial} \times 1,000 \div \text{number of households}$$

The rates for air time are established by the number of viewers. Thus, prime-time spots are more expensive than are late-night spots.

MEASURING AUDIENCES

TV viewing on stations across the country is measured by four methods.

1. *Electronic recorder.* This technique was developed by the A. C. Nielsen Company. It uses an electronic measuring device that, when attached to the TV set, automatically records the channel to which the set is tuned and the length of time it is on. The taped records are sent to a panel of members

each week. The panel compares the tapes against the rosters of known stations and programs to arrive at a national rating for each program.

2. *Telephone coincidental.* This is one of the earliest methods of measuring audiences, with its beginnings in radio. An interviewer calls a household selected at random and asks to which TV show they are tuned. With this method, coverage is limited, but results are obtained quickly.

3. *Diary method.* Selected households are asked to keep diaries of each program they watch. It is a simple, inexpensive method. Both A. C. Nielsen and Arbitron provide diary services that measure station and program delivery in more than 200 major markets.

4. *Roster recall.* In this method, door-to-door surveys are conducted. The interviewer carries a list of programs that were broadcast the day before and asks each household member to scan the list during the interview.

THE STORYBOARD

The visual idea of a commercial is called a *storyboard*. A storyboard is made on a piece of sturdy posterboard large enough to contain the artwork that shows the sequence of the commercial. The visual changes are shown in *frames*. A frame represents one-thirtieth of a second of the commercial. The main function of the storyboard is to illustrate the commercial's content before it goes into production. The storyboard is the compete visualization of the idea for the commercial.

A storyboard is rather like a blueprint in that it is subject to refinement along the way. Changes can be made before production begins according to directions from the advertiser, the agency people, or the director of the commercial.

As a rule, the commercial will be represented in about eight frames. The commercial's script, camera effects, and background music are oftentimes noted on the storyboard.

Once there is agreement that the proposed ad conveys the desired message, it is turned over to a director.

The film director transforms the storyboard into live, flowing motion. He or she will instinctively determine optical and technical effects, using camera and lights to enhance the commercial's effect.

While many large retail operations contain in-house production centers, most production is handled by outside agencies which supply crews and equipment as well as studio facilities. Some local television stations provide production facilities to their advertisers, and high-quality commercials can be made at low cost in this manner. A major advertiser's network commercial may cost $50,000 to produce. Yet a good commercial can be produced for as little as $500.

The actual filming of a commercial is similar to condensing an entire playlet into 30 or 60 seconds. The commercial is presented as a "story" that has a beginning, middle, and end. Whether it demonstrates a "hot" fashion item or promotes a storewide sale or promotional event, the action must move fast to make an impression on the viewer. Characters and plot must be established from the start.

The producer, director, and file crew bring the script, music, and action together as indicated on the storyboard. Changes along the way are subject to the director's interpretation at the time of filming.

The more elaborate the production, the higher the cost. If professional actors are needed, a cast must be selected and rehearsed. If the script calls for an outdoor location, a location service may be retained to find the right spot. Location settings may require transportation, extra personnel, and equipment, all of which adds to the cost. Background music when used can be either "canned" (tape recorded) or performed live and then edited into the finished product.

Summary

A medium of sight, sound, and motion, television is a powerful tool for fashion retailers. Versatile and flexible, the TV ad can be used to project or change store image or to promote and showcase merchandise—providing the viewer with close-up details of an item's special features. Television delivers a wide audience and enables the retailer to deliver a message simultaneously to the viewer's sense of sight and sound, thereby increasing the impact of the message and the chances of response.

In the media mix, the TV ad is used to support advertising carried in the other media; it may, in fact, reach target customers that were missed through other advertising efforts. Once too expensive for all but the large retailer with an equal-ly large budget, television advertising is now available to most fashion retailers due to the growth of cable television, which offers targeted local coverage at a low cost.

Terms for Review

1. Infomercials
2. Static ad
3. Prime time
4. Network

5. Local broadcasts
6. Cost per thousand
7. Storyboard
8. Frame

Study Review Questions

1. Why is television considered a powerful and influential medium?
2. Explain the effect cable television has had on the retailer.
3. Why would the TV ad be effective in changing store image?
4. In what way can a TV ad affect mood?
5. How do manufacturers encourage the use of television as an advertising vehicle?

6. Why would a retailer have to run the television ad more than once?
7. Why would network ad time appeal to a large retailer? Explain why a network ad would not be a good choice for the small retailer.

Case

Somewhere Specialty is a small retailer that carries both men's and women's sportswear. The store's customer base comprises young professionals. Recently, the owner decided to add an infant and children's clothing department.

Questions

1. Who should the owner target for the new department?
2. What media mix would you recommend?
3. What role would television play in the Somewhere Specialty sales promotion campaign?

12 OTHER ADVERTISING METHODS

We have examined the various mass media used by the fashion retailer to communicate with the store's target customer. Newspapers, radio, and television each has its place in the media mix, each has a slightly different role in delivering the message the retailer seeks to convey to the customer the store seeks to attract.

In this chapter we will examine other methods of conveying that message. Some of these methods enable the retailer to more precisely target the customer and customize the message; others take more of a shot-gun approach—it is not as easy to quantify the reach, the ability to target the message, or customer recall of these methods of advertising.

Every retailer with an eye on growth and profitability conducts an ongoing pursuit of new marketing techniques: (1) to penetrate new areas of profit; (2) to keep pace with competitors; and (3) to add greater dimension to the marketing plan, thereby increasing its overall effectiveness.

Broadly, *direct advertising* is any kind of advertising that is delivered directly to a chosen prospect. It can come through the mail, be inserted into newspapers, handed to the prospect by a salesperson, delivered to the prospect by a distribution service, or, with recent advances in technology, through the prospect's computer via CD-ROM or on-line services.

Direct mail refers to any advertising that is sent through the U.S. postal service. A catalog sent by a department store is direct mail. If the same catalog is inserted in the Sunday newspaper, it is no longer direct mail but direct advertising.

Mail-order advertising is not an advertising medium in itself but a method by which the customer can order a product. Mail-order advertising uses the various media, particularly direct mail, magazines, and newspapers. It is also a misnomer; with the proliferation of credit cards and 800 numbers, the customer is just as likely to phone in the order for merchandise.

Number of Americans Who Shop at Home

Year	Total Adult Population	Number (millions) Shopped Direct	Percentage of Population
1994	187.7	98.5	52.5
1993	185.8	97.7	52.6
1992	184.0	101.6	55.2
1991	181.1	96.0	52.6
1990	181.1	98.6	54.4
1989	178.2	91.7	51.4
1988	173.7	88.5	51.0
1987	169.5	88.0	52.0
1986	169.5	87.7	52.0
1985	164.9	76.2	46.2
1984	161.9	64.4	40.0
1983	158.4	57.4	36.2

Figure 12.1

The number of Americans who shop from home has drastically increased in recent years. Courtesy of Direct Marketing Association, Inc.

Direct Mail

According to the Direct Marketing Association, Inc., direct-mail advertising increased nearly 150% from 1983 ($11.79 billion) to 1993 ($27.43 billion). Direct mail's share of the total advertising dollars spent in America also increased, from 15.6% in 1983 to 19.9% in 1993.

Why the increase? Simply put, direct mail works.

As exhibited in Figure 12.1, the Direct Marketing Association reports that in 1994 the number of Americans who shopped at home by mail or by phone totaled 98.5 million. In other words, 52.5% of the total U.S. adult population purchased merchandise from home.

The theories to explain the trend are many. Some point to the increased numbers of women who work, others to the hectic pace of modern life which leaves little time to shop at retail stores. Theories are offered that the nation is in a cocooning stage. Still others attribute the proliferation of credit cards, 800 numbers, and increased efficiency and reach of delivery services. Whatever the reasons behind it, shopping at home has become accepted and big business.

The term "direct mail" can apply to a number of vehicles used to carry advertising through the mail, from the postcard to the voluminous catalog. The method is limited only by the budget of the direct-mail marketer. The following are some of the most common direct-mail vehicles.

Catalogs.   Mail-order houses and most department and specialty stores regularly send out booklets consisting of many pages which illustrate their merchandise. These *catalogs* are usually printed in color on good-quality paper. In design and size they closely resemble magazines. Catalogs are carefully merchandised and are commonly used in connection with holiday promotions, a storewide sale, or at the beginning of the new selling season.

   We can gain insight into the marketing power of the catalog from the results of the Direct Marketing Association's "Impact of Direct Marketing on the American Economy" study. Conducted by The WEFA Group, an econometric modeling and forecasting firm, the study found catalog revenue had reached $53.4 billion in sales in 1993—an average growth of nearly 7% per year from $35.7 billion in sales in 1987. The study forecasted catalog sales revenue will grow an average of 6.8% annually to reach 69.5 billion by 1997.

Sales Letters.   These are generally sent to customers to announce an event, such as a sale, or a service provided by the store. *Sales letters* are often printed on the store's stationery with the logo as the letterhead. The salutation is commonly personalized, addressing the customer by name. Sales letters are a personal and inexpensive form of advertising that requires only the cost of duplication and mailing.

Postcards.   Another inexpensive method is the printed *postcard*. This is useful for sending brief advertising notices and requires only third-class postage. Because its cost is modest, this form of advertising is practical for frequent mailings.

Statement Enclosures.   Single-page or one-fold leaflets can be used to alert the customer to special purchases or new products. The message may be merely printed or may be illustrated in color. *Statement enclosures* are economical since they ride free with the customer's monthly bill (providing that the total mailing weight is one ounce or less). These enclosures, sometimes referred to as "stuffers," often carry an order form which can be filled out and returned with payment of the bill in an enclosed postage-paid envelope.

Self-mailing Folders.   *Self-mailers* are larger than statement enclosures. Heavier paper is required, since the self-mailer goes through the mail without an envelope. The self-mailer folds twice or more and can carry illustrations, text, or a combination of both.

Broadsides.   The *broadside* is a folded self-mailer used to deliver a continuous selling message as it unfolds. Because of its size, it lends itself to detailed description and graphic demonstration of a product. The aim of the broadside is to impress the customer with its size and content.

Retailers and Direct Mail

Although it is not considered a mass medium, direct mail claims a substantial portion of the retail advertising budget in department and specialty stores. There are few retailers who have not used direct mail in one form or another.

Direct mail offers the retailer the following distinct advantages over other forms of direct advertising.

Selectivity.   Coverage can be as specific as desired. Customer demographics and psychographics determined by survey research are available from list specialists. Prospect names can be selectively pulled from computer files. Most retailers possess the basic capabilities to build their own customer and prospect lists.

Flexibility.   Costs of direct-mail advertising can be controlled more readily than in other media. There is a broad choice of formats, from simple leaflets inserted in monthly statements to commanding catalogs, depending upon the budget.

Personal Contact.   Direct mail can be a one-to-one communication by addressing the receiver by name through the privacy of mail. In broadcast and print media, an advertisement is subject to dilution and comparison with competitor's ads, while direct mail, if read, receives the concentrated attention of the prospective customer.

Direct mail has, however, limitations. It is difficult to obtain the perfect list. Even though lists are continually refined and updated, there is no ironclad way to guarantee that they will correctly pinpoint the desired target. Additionally, the direct-mail piece must compete with quantities of other mail to be read.

A direct-mail effort could be as simple as letting the regular store customer know that merchandise has arrived, or it can be used as an element of a sales promotion campaign of image repositioning. For the fashion retailer, the catalog is a common direct-mail vehicle and represents the largest direct-mail investment. Major department and specialty stores produce seasonal or sales catalogs which are primarily mailed to charge customers. The annual Christmas catalog is the most important mailer of the year, coinciding with the selling period during which stores register approximately one-third of their annual sales.

Figure 12.2 is an example of a simple postcard effort that accomplishes several purposes. First, let's look at the promotional aspects of the mailing. The direct-mail piece alerts the store's regular customers that boots have arrived in the store. The postcard lists the prices of the boots offered, reminds the customer of the store's "already low boot prices," and provides an additional enticement—a $2.00 discount.

But this direct-mail effort is also institutional in nature, enhancing the image of the store. The mailing is a welcomed reminder; in the demanding world of parenthood, a forewarning of an upcoming need is appreciated. More important,

Trade in Boot Sale

Take $2.00 off our already low boot prices when you
trade in a pair of used work boots or winter boots.
(No holes, please) All boots will be donated to charity.

Lacrosse 100% Waterproof Boots	$19.99 – 2.00 off
Brown Duck Boot	26.00 – 2.00 off
Look Boots for Mom	
Navy Duck boot	26.00 – 2.00 off
*Baby's Snowboot	19.99 – 2.00 off
**Tan Workboot (like Dad's)	26.00 – 2.00 off
Pink Bubblegummers Workboot	27.00 – 2.00 off
Black Bubblegummers Workboot	27.00 – 2.00 off

*Delivery Date: October 20th (please call first)
**Delivery Date: October 17th (please call first)

SHOESTRINGS

428 Main Street, Palmer, MA 01069 • 283-4940
HOURS: Mon-Wed 10-5 / Thurs 10-7 / Fri 10-5 / Sat 10-4

Figure 12.2

Even a simple postcard can be used to meet promotional and institutional advertising objectives. Courtesy of SHOESTRINGS, Palmer, MA.

SHOESTRINGS projects itself as a caring member of the community through its offer to accept used boots that will then be donated to charity.

An example of how direct mail can be used to reposition a store and attract new business is the 1993 ECHO entry—I. Magnin's "A New Attitude" campaign. The ECHO Awards, an annual international competition sponsored by the Direct Marketing Association, recognize excellence in direct-response advertising on the basis of measured response, marketing strategy, and creativity.

I. Magnin used its spring catalog, featuring upscale female apparel with price points ranging from $25.00 to $1,000.00, to launch the store's new advertising campaign entitled "A New Attitude." The major objective of the retailer's sales promotion campaign was to attract a new, younger customer; the retailer also wanted to reach the past customer. The latest in designer fashion was the bait for the campaign's objectives.

The catalog campaign was targeted to a narrow segment of the mail-order population—upscale female apparel mail-order buyers with an average order of $200; the circulation comprised the store's house file and rented lists with the same demographic parameters. I. Magnin credit cardholders were also targeted to promote store traffic.

The 1.3 million catalogs mailed contained the "A New Attitude" logo throughout the magazinelike format, which included heavier matt paper stock, editorials, and black-and-white photography. The gross cost of the effort, including creative, preproduction, production, media support, and postage was $1,009,481.00.

The direct-mail campaign met its objective of a 1% response rate, and reportedly store traffic also increased. With the average sale at $274.00, the retailer estimated the campaign cost at $2.85 per customer.

As you can see, direct mail offers the retailer a variety of options with a range of associated costs. It is a medium that can be deployed to fit the individual retailer's budget and objectives.

DIRECT-MARKETING DIVISIONS

Several merchants consider direct-mail marketing so important to the store that they have established direct-marketing divisions separate from the other sales promotion divisions within the store. The sole function of the division is to handle direct mail. As such, the division interacts with the store buyers who select the merchandise to be marketed. The division usually has no control over the merchandise to be shown in the catalog; however, it may edit the selection.

According to individual policy, merchandise shown in the catalog may also be available in the store, but in some cases the buyer will purchase a small percentage of items for catalog selling only.

MAIL-ORDER MARKETERS

Mail-order houses sell merchandise by catalog only. Their catalogs are sent to prospects whose names have been purchased from *list houses,* which are in the business of collecting and selling names and addresses of people at various economic levels and with defined demographic profiles.

Catalogs sell virtually anything that can be packaged and shipped; the items sold through catalogs range from stationery supplies to food items, from garden tools to designer apparel.

While the Sears, Roebuck and Co. "Big Book" catalog—the grandfather of all direct marketing—offered virtually all merchandise classifications, the current trend is for catalog merchandise to be focused on specific classifications. That is to say, most catalogs specialize in a particular theme of merchandise and items closely related to it, much like the retail specialty store. Some blamed the Sears catalog's lack of specialty focus for its demise in 1993. Perhaps, but as identified earlier, the only constant in the world of retailing is change.

Let's look at the history of Lands' End, an international direct merchant of "cut and sewn" products. Founded in 1963, Lands' End initially supplied sailboat hardware and equipment by mail. (The company says that the misplaced apostrophe in the logo can be traced to a typo in the first printed piece, which it says it couldn't afford to reprint and correct.) Lands' End's early catalogs included clothing to complement other products. The company decided to focus its efforts on selling clothing and soft luggage in 1976.

The core of Lands' End's business is what the company calls its primary catalog, as illustrated in Figure 12.3. Mailed every four weeks, the primary catalog averages 160 pages and offers a full line of traditionally styled, classic casual apparel for men and women, as well as accessories and soft luggage. The "prospect catalog" is designed to turn nonbuyers into buyers. Mailed several times a year to names from its own house file and from purchased lists, this direct-mail effort averages 64 pages and focuses on the merchant's best-selling items.

Lands' End further narrows its sales promotion efforts with four specialty catalogs: "Kids," casual clothing for children and infants; "Coming Home," quality bedding and bath items; "Beyond Buttondowns," tailored clothing for men; and "Textures," tailored clothing for the working woman.

Today there are approximately 7.4 million Lands' End customers throughout the United States, Canada, and the world; the company's net income for fiscal 1994 was $42.4 million on net sales of $870 million.

MAILING LISTS

The most important component of the mail-order campaign is the names and addresses of individuals or households to which the mailing will be sent. Tremendous investments are made in producing impressive mailings, but these expenditures are wasted unless the direct-mail marketer possesses a mailing list of likely prospects for the merchandise offered. In order for a list to be successful, there must be a logical connection between the product offered and the prospects. This is sometimes referred to as *list affinity.*

LIST CATEGORIES

There are four broad categories of lists in direct-mail marketing: *response lists, compiled lists, business lists,* and *house lists.*

Response Lists.   These are the names of buyers, subscribers, donors, members, or depositors who have previously responded to a direct-marketing offer. This is the basic type of list used in consumer direct mail.

Compiled Lists.   These are lists of names that have been collected from telephone books, directories, membership lists, and other similar sources. The characteristic of these lists is that there is no indication that these people have ever responded to a direct-mail offer.

Business Lists.   Lists of this kind are used for business-to-business selling rather than consumer selling. Originally, business lists were compiled from Yellow Pages directories. Now they are more easily compiled from coded lists published by the U.S. Government Office of Statistical Standards. Each type of

Figure 12.3

Lands' End includes "direct merchants" as part of its logo—a more accurate description of this market segment considering the number of customers who now use the telephone instead of the mail to place orders. In addition, since Lands' End has already begun to test on-line service, CD-ROM, and the interactive kiosk as alternative avenues of reaching and serving its customers, direct merchants—instead of mail-order house—more accurately describes this company and possibly a future segment of the retailing industry. Courtesy of Lands' End, Inc.

business has its own code number, called a Standard Industrial Classification (SIC code).

House Lists.   These are lists composed of a company's own clients. In the case of a retailer, a house list is compiled from its charge customers.

HOW LISTS ARE OBTAINED

There are several ways that direct-mail marketers obtain their lists.

1. They can be purchased or rented from list brokers (see Figure 12.4).
2. They can be exchanged with other list holders.
3. They can be compiled from store accounts and other relevant sources.

Lists can be broadly general or highly selective, according to the needs of the direct-mail marketer. Specific profiles can be obtained; these are described by demographics (sex, marital status, household income, family size, and so on) or can be more finely described by psychographics (interests, values, and preferences of the individuals).

With the proliferation of personal computers, almost any retailer has the capacity to maintain extensive house lists called *databases.* Increasingly, retailers are using databases and *database marketing* to improve their advertising efficiency and for making marketing and merchandising decisions.

The typical database would consist of the customer's name, address, and purchases. These names can be recalled at will for use in targeted direct-mail campaigns. In addition to avoiding waste, by targeting those customers who will likely respond, databases can be used to analyze results—by tracking how the customer responds—that can be employed in future planning efforts.

For example, a store could send a special mailer only to women who spend over $2,000 a year in the store; the computer is commanded to recall and print out just those customer names. Or, a postcard promoting a sale on men's shirts and accessories could be targeted only to customers who recently purchased a men's suit.

Database marketing is also being used by retailers to generate new customers. Again, the ability to target a select audience, in effect have a dialogue with the customer the store wants to attract, is the advantage of database marketing.

Kay-Bee Toy Stores used database marketing to launch *GoodTimes,* a magazine featuring articles for adults and for children accompanied by ads and coupons from toy makers and other marketers. The mailing list comprised families with children aged 4 to 14 living within a 10-minute drive of a Kay-Bee store. While it cost the company $2 million to produce and mail the magazine, company officials were reportedly pleased with the results, calling it cost effective. An independent reader research company found that all of the surveyed households that received the magazine said that they had read it. Some 59% of

Figure 12.4

Lists that match the customer to the product can be purchased from companies that specialize in finding the right names. Courtesy of AZ List Managers.

the readers bought an advertised product and the overall average recall for seeing ads was 63%.

The small retailer, whose budget may not allow for the purchase of outside lists, can turn to other sources to build effective, targeted lists of prospective customers, including:

1. Lists from local associations
2. Directories: telephone books, city directories, Chamber of Commerce directories, and professional and trade directories
3. Newspaper announcements of births, marriages, relocations, and home purchases

For a list to have any value, it must deliver a profitable rate of response to mailings. There are many sophisticated mathematical methods of determining profitability for the various types of mail-order campaigns. One simple way used to examine the progress of a campaign is to determine the cost per response (CPR), or what a mailer costs for each response that is received for it. This is arrived at by dividing the cost of the entire promotion by the total number of responses.

$$\text{promotion cost} \div \text{number of responses} = \text{cost per response}$$

Lists are often tested to determine the potential success of a mail-order campaign. For example, prior to sending a mailing to 10,000 prospects, a retailer might send a premail testing of 1,000 sample names to get an indication of the response. The reason for the test is obviously to limit the risk. If a test mailing to the sample produces the desired response, it is then probable that the rest of the list will give the same result.

Computerized Nonstore Marketing

We have already identified that the technology is available to enable a customer to interact with the home television. This technology would involve a keyboard attached to the set, enabling the customer to enter the order, personal measurements, and a credit card number.

Other advances in this area appear daily. The CD-ROM has provided retailers with another avenue to display their goods and reach a potential customer. The Internet—or "Information Super Highway" as it is sometimes called—is another outlet being tested by retailers. The medium has had a slow start; customers have shown resistance to sending their credit cards numbers through the system on E-mail, and limitations in the technology has prompted critics to call the Internet "a poor shop window." Still, adventurous retailers are blazing the trail on this increasingly common technology, offering everything from apparel to books, from flowers to travel services.

On-line shopping may someday be commonplace. Proponents argue that the reign of the paper catalog may be ending. Environmental and conservation concerns may serve to make the deluge of catalogs unwelcome; this and a concern for privacy, they argue, are the reasons behind the increasing numbers of people requesting that their names be removed from mailing lists.

Magazines

In general, it is the manufacturer rather than the retailer who advertises most widely in magazines. Manufacturers, in fact, place more advertising in magazines than in any other medium. The retailer ultimately benefits from the advertising barrage since customers who are familiar with a manufacturer's brand are more inclined to purchase the product at retail.

Large retailers do use magazine advertising to obtain national exposure. The paper stock used in magazines is superior to newsprint, and the reproduction quality is far superior, enabling the retailer to place a dramatic advertisement. The object of these institutional ads is to build the prestige image of the store instead of selling a specific item. In today's world of extensive business and pleasure travel, the magazine advertising expenditure makes sense; the visitor to a strange city is attracted immediately to a store with a familiar name.

Magazines are broadly classed by the audience they reach. Consumer magazines are read by the ultimate consumer and are considered general-interest magazines. This classification is broken down further to define the magazine according to its main focus. Thus, *Sports Illustrated, Family Circle,* and *Vogue* are, respectively, classified as a sports news magazine, service magazine, and fashion magazine.

There are other magazines that the ultimate consumer reads, but they are more narrow in focus and classification. Business magazines focus on the conduct of business and the economy, trade magazines focus on a select business group, and professional journals are directed toward a particular professional group such as doctors or lawyers. As the magazine's focus narrows, the number of people in the magazine's audience grows smaller and more select. While targeting a finite select audience is appropriate for some advertisers, retailers generally stick with magazines with wider appeal.

Magazines are published on a weekly, monthly, bimonthly, or quarterly basis. Generally, the cover price of a monthly magazine is higher than that of a weekly, and the reader tends to retain the issue longer, rereading it or passing it to another person. For that reason, retailers tend to use the monthly publications in order to get more for their advertising investment.

National magazines often subdivide their distribution into regional issues, enabling a retailer to place an ad that will be seen in a particular region of the country. Another way retailers achieve a more localized geographic exposure in their magazine advertising is by placing an ad in a regional magazine or publication that caters in content and distribution to a certain geographic area.

The method of distribution the magazine uses is also a consideration for the retailer. Magazines are sold by subscription and over the counter at newsstands, supermarkets racks, and so on. Magazines with a high percentage of subscription copies make more sense for the retailer, since the audience for the ad is better defined and guaranteed.

Figure 12.5
Out-of-home advertising gives the retailer reach and frequency at a low cost.
Courtesy of the Institute for Outdoor Advertising.

Out-of-Home Advertising

Out-of-home advertising comprises advertising outside the home or office, including billboards, as in Figure 12.5, posters in transit stations and on the side of buses, ads on the sides of bus shelters and phone kiosks, and even paintings on sides of skyscrapers and construction sites.

While outdoor advertising may be the oldest advertising medium, the increased interest of the fashion industry is news. Familiar fixtures on the out-of-home scene include names from Calvin Klein and Donna Karen to Levi's jeans, from Neiman Marcus to Benetton and the Gap. According to the Outdoor Advertising Association of America, the retail industry spent $152 million in 1993—not including spending for transit advertising, the fastest-growing segment of the industry—doubling the amount spent the year before for outdoor advertising.

The Outdoor Advertising Association of America describes the medium as "big, bold, and hard to ignore." One of the advantages of out-of-home advertising is its ability to communicate with the dramatic impact of size and color. Since it is "transmitting" the message all day, every day, out-of-home rapidly builds reach and frequency.

It is also cost effective. Industry experts compare the cost of out-of-home advertising—as little as $1.00 a day to reach 1,000 people—with $3.00 for radio and newspapers and $7.50 for television. The cost to lease a billboard for a month in the New York market—$20,000—is still only half the amount some fashion magazines charge for a full page ad.

The medium even supplies the advertiser with the ability to target the audience for the communication. For example, by choosing specific bus routes, or utilizing phone kiosks in the nightclub section of a city, advertisers have the ability to determine who will see the ad.

Store Packaging

While this area is often overlooked, especially by small retailers, the containers the store provides the customer to carry purchased merchandise from the store—boxes, bags, and shopping bags—are yet another vehicle to advertise the store. Often reused, a shopping bag with the store's logo on it is similar to a moving billboard; the customer is in effect endorsing the store to the general public.

Some stores have utilized this medium so effectively, as is the case in the aforementioned striped packaging of Henri Bendel, that the design of the packaging serves a role equal to the store logo.

Summary

Direct mail takes many forms: catalogs, sales letters, postcards, stuffers, self-mailing folders, and broadsides. The success of direct mail depends on selective lists of prospects which are rented, purchased, or drawn from the store's own computer database and supplemented from other sources.

Out-of-home advertising includes transit advertising and rented space on billboards, telephone kiosks, even the sides of buildings. The fashion industry has recently increased the expenditures on this medium, largely due to its ability to deliver targeted audiences at low CPM and production costs.

Finally, the retailer cannot afford to miss an opportunity to advertise the store and build the store's image. Even the retailer's packaging plays a role in reaching the store's target customer.

Terms for Review

1. Direct advertising
2. Direct mail
3. Mail-order advertising
4. Catalogs
5. Sales letters
6. Postcards
7. Statement enclosures
8. Self-mailers
9. Broadsides
10. List house
11. List affinity
12. Response lists
13. Compiled lists
14. Business lists
15. House lists
16. Database
17. Database marketing
18. Out-of-home advertising

Study Review Questions

1. Describe the difference between direct advertising and direct mail.
2. Why is mail-order advertising a misnomer?
3. What factors have had an effect on direct-mail advertising?
4. What is list affinity?
5. How are direct-mailing lists obtained?
6. How and why are mailing lists tested?
7. Explain how the proliferation of personal computers has had an impact on fashion sales promotion.
8. What is CPR and how is it used?
9. How would a manufacturer's ad in a magazine benefit the retailer?
10. Explain how out-of-home advertising is said to rapidly build reach and frequency.

Case

Anyplace Department Store has decided to buy a bulletin ad space on the interstate highway that passes the city in which the store is located. It has contracted the space for $1,000 a month for three months. The advertising director plans to use the space for three ads: an institutional the first month, a summer sale in the next, and an ad featuring fall merchandise as the last.

Questions

1. Describe the likely reader of the ad.
2. How does the medium used affect the ad's content and style?
3. Discuss the limitations the ad director faces in the last ad.

13 VISUAL MERCHANDISING: Another Dimension

We have talked about advertising and the way in which the different media are used to bring customers into the store and generate sales.

Visual merchandising is an aspect of sales promotion that is both nonpersonal and personal. It is nonpersonal in that it is not a two-way communication; it is personal in that it is the element of sales promotion that is directed at the customers' senses—sight, touch, sound, even smell.

Visual merchandising is the vehicle that the retailer uses to capture the customer at the point of purchase. From the design of the store's exterior and interior layout to its windows and point-of-sale displays, the retailer employs visual merchandising to communicate with the customer. Visual merchandising communicates the store's image, reinforces the store's advertising efforts, and prompts the need-to-buy impulse.

Visual merchandising creates the environment in which to display the goods offered for sale. It is used to educate, to inform, to entertain, to set the mood. It is through this element of sales promotion that the store's true character and personality are communicated.

As with other aspects of sales promotion, visual merchandising can be promotional in nature or institutional in purpose. The rules that govern all aspects of sales promotion apply here: to be effective, visual merchandising must reflect and address the target customer's needs and desires. Otherwise, this form of sales promotion communication fails.

Merchandising through visual merchandising is the most dynamic route to sales. It is a powerful form of show-and-tell, even though not a word is spoken.

While most of this chapter will deal with the more traditional definitions of display—window, interior display, and so on—a mention of the interior design of the store itself, and the role it plays in visual merchandising, is necessary.

The layout of the store, the materials used for floors, walls, and dividers, even the size and decor of the dressing rooms all combine to create and project the store's image. Specialty retailers often hire architects to ensure that the design of the store projects the retailer's desired image. Architectural elements of space, flow, lighting, and materials are taken into consideration. This prototype design is then adapted for each store in the chain. That is why as customers we "recognize" a store as we approach, even if this branch location is new to us. The physical look of the retailer is part of its signature—much like its logo.

While department stores are less flexible when it comes to the physical design of an existing building, departments within the store are periodically redecorated to create a specific mood or image for the merchandise offered there. As the customer steps into a department from the traffic isle, floor coverings, wall coverings, lighting, and the use of color all indicate the type of merchandise contained within that section of the store.

The point is that the physical surroundings are an important element in visual merchandising.

The facade of the store in Figure 13.1 provides maximum visual impact. The interior of World Foot Locker store in fact becomes the store's exterior. Borrowing from the sports arena and the out-of-doors, the store is designed to provide the customer with a fast-paced and efficient shopping experience.

Figure 13.1

The World Foot Locker's interior is, in effect, the store's exterior. Courtesy of the Athletic Specialty Division of Woolworth Corporation.

The sports theme is carried throughout the design of the store. The nonskid flooring takes its inspiration from a track, with concentric circles of stone aggregate. The unfinished ceiling is painted deep blue, and stretched fabric panels suggest an outdoor, tentlike structure. Even the overhead ducts, usually hidden from view, are wrapped like padded stadium surfaces. This theme is continued with stadium-like, metal halide fixtures to supplement the halogen, incandescent, and fluorescent light sources.

Two 10-foot 6-inch athletic sentries flank the entrance to the store. A double-sided basketball hoop hangs over the circular service desk. Even a support beam in the front of the store performs an image function: it acts as a display case for baseballs.

The World Foot Locker example illustrates the powerful role the physical design of the store plays in visual merchandising.

Types of Displays and What They Do

The store's fashion philosophy is evidenced in its displays, its merchandise selection, its interior design, and even its housekeeping.

When a customer walks into Bloomingdale's, New York, the implicit message one receives from the visual merchandising is "We are young and on the go— we are in the fashion vanguard."

A few blocks west at Bergdorf Goodman, the message is unmistakably "Tasteful elegance—top of the line—luxury."

The message is delivered by exploiting our emotions and our senses through three-dimensional *exterior* and *interior displays.* Most of us are unaware that the influences on our shopping behavior are orchestrated by experienced marketing professionals. This does not necessarily mean that the customer is totally devoid of will. The finest visual presentation on earth cannot create loyal customers if quality and value are missing.

WINDOW DISPLAY

If you measure your attention span while standing before a window, you will find that it is only a matter of seconds before you move on or enter the store. An analogy can be made with selecting a TV channel; if your interest is not engaged in those first crucial moments, you switch the channels.

The object of the window is to motivate you toward a closer look at the merchandise and to plant the yearning to buy. The window tells a story that is constructed much as a news article in that it employs the age-old "five Ws"—who, what, why, when, where. It says, here is the latest fashion; this is the way to put it together; this is where and when to wear the look; this is an image with which you can identify.

All this comes into play in window arrangements, from the simplest to the most complex. But in addition to being informational, windows have become an art form which at best reach the level of theater.

Whether the window is fashion oriented, institutional, or promotional in nature, it is most successful when it adheres to a dominant theme. Some of the treatments that may be used include:

- A single mannequin against seamless paper
- A realistic setting peopled with a group of mannequins in action
- A theatrical setting, an injection of fantasy and drama
- Animation, as in holiday windows that draw crowds of viewers
- Use of sculpture, fine painting reproductions, or art objects
- Media tie-ins with current films, stars, or best-selling books

As with all aspects of sales promotion, the window "message" must be appropriate to the customer the store seeks to attract through its doors.

In most major urban areas, where pedestrian traffic is heavy, retail windows carry great weight. In suburban branch stores or malls where customers must enter the store through underground parking areas or mall entrances, window space is usually limited. Here, exterior display takes a back seat to interior display.

Windows are planned to integrate with their entire surroundings. The window designer creates a "whole" rather than a fragment, taking into consideration the building facade, the street and its people, and the relationships of perspective, color harmonies, lighting, and viewing angle.

Even the design of the windows themselves influence how they are treated and the visual merchandising role they play.

With large plate glass fronts, the *closed-back* window is most common to older shopping districts. The remaining three walls are enclosed, creating a protected theater in which the visual merchandising story can unfold.

Its origin in this country is traced back to 1862, when New York City's A. T. Stewart's plate glass windows gave birth to the outdoor sport of window shopping.

While access to the closed-back window is commonly through a door or sliding panel, Lord & Taylor's Fifth Avenue store has a unique feature. The window floors are on hydraulic lifts. When it is time to change the window display, the floor of the window is lowered into the display department's work area.

The closed-back window allows for maximum creativity and theater. The window display, comprising merchandise and props, is protected—there is no worry that the display will be tampered with.

Since the back walls block the view into the store, the display in this type of window does not have to compete with the view of the store's interior. Conversely, this type of window is more expensive to maintain and to merchandise precisely for the same reason. Since the customer has no other view of what the store has to offer, the visual merchandising responsibility—to draw the customer in—is greater for this type of window.

At the other end of the spectrum is the *open-back* window. In this case the display in the window functions to stop the passerby and then draw the eye to the store's interior.

While the visual merchandising demands would seemingly be less, effective display for this type of window has its challenges and limitations.

Since the display is fully accessible, and the back of the display is in full view from inside the store, both technical and practical considerations abound. The display must work with and complement the merchandise displayed in the store; the display is likely to be touched and tampered with; technical concerns of lighting, securing the props used, and even how to hide such mundane items as pins and wires are increased with this type of window.

Some of these concerns are mitigated by the addition of a partial divider. The divider in the *partially open* window can be horizontal or vertical; the interior of the store is still visible, but the window has more definition.

The degree of separation between window and store interior depends on the partition used. For example, a horizontal divider—a wrought iron or wood fence—provides full view of the store's interior while providing display protection and window space definition. A vertical divider—a mural or draped fabric—trades a clear view of the store's interior for more window function in the visual merchandising sense.

A *shadow-box* window is small, elevated, and shallow. Ideal for small item displays, the shadow-box window also provides maximum security. Security is also a feature of the *island window,* which, just as its name implies, is a display enclosed on all sides in glass.

Finally, as we have seen in Figure 13.1, the "window" to the store may be the store itself.

INTERIOR DISPLAY

As the customer enters the store, displays continue to beat out the fashion message. While windows are designed to stop traffic, interior displays are designed to guide the shopper to the point of sale. There are a number of ways for doing so: floor displays, department or "shop" displays, point-of-sale displays, signs, and fixturing.

Interior display is an integral part of the architectural design and floor plan of the store. You will note in Figure 13.2, an interior shot of the World Foot Locker store, that the store's design includes perimeter walls merchandised from floor to ceiling.

Display combines with traffic patterns to guide the customers through the store. Visual merchandising enables the customer to select merchandise easily from what might otherwise be a jumble of goods.

A window is rather like a tableau. It has boundaries within which the designer creates. The interior display designer is not locked into a static area but must utilize existing space directly on the selling floor at strategic spots where traffic is the heaviest, such as the entrance, escalator and elevator banks, and stairways.

Interior displays must also be versatile, easily assembled, and disassembled. The designer avoids crowding or positioning that may create a safety hazard.

Interiors are changed often in order to continually stimulate sales. If necessary, interior displays are changed as often as twice a week, particularly in areas where sales are sluggish. This may entail moving new merchandise forward, rearranging displays to give merchandise a fresh look, or placing other merchandise at the rear of the department.

When setting up a display, the designer considers *adjacencies*, or the effect the display will have on the department directly next to it. Ideally, the displays are merchandised to draw the customer from one area to the next, increasing sales.

Interior displays do not have to be elaborate to be effective. Take a peek at Figure 13.3. The fixture in the foreground of the photo performs double duty. By design it is both a means to create an interior display and to display merchandise. The way in which the fixture was used makes it much more than a merchandise "rack."

The limited edition jackets are not intended to be a large-volume item; their presence has more to do with visual merchandising, fashion, and store image than with potential sales volume. The simple placement of two athletic shoes on the top platform of the rack is more than decorative—it serves to "remind" the customer, to draw the customer to that merchandise.

The best interior displays feature merchandise above all, avoiding the props that could dilute the fashion statement the store is trying to make.

Elements of Visual Display

An outstanding window or interior display got that way because a true professional designed it. If you admire a display and respond to it emotionally, there is a reason for it. The merchandise should be the first thing you see. But the overall color scheme, the proportion, and balance of the display affects you aesthetically, just as well-designed painting or piece of sculpture would.

The designer-as-artist attempts to achieve the very ultimate in good design principles in order to elicit your response. The display designer creates with these basic materials: the all-important merchandise, mannequins, background textures, props, and lighting. In assembling all this into a creditable piece of display work, basic design principles are applied.

Whether or not you recognize them right off the bat, if you have done a double take at an exciting display, these principles are operating:

Color.   Color is the most important element in the designer's arsenal. Harmony is achieved with two or more colors that are similar. For instance, red and orange are related on the color wheel because orange is a combination of red and yellow.

Line.   Direction, implied by the stance of a mannequin or the shape of architectural background elements, lends a mood. Diagonals suggest energy and motion. Horizontals imply restfulness. Verticals are stately, strong.

Conflict. Straight lines are played against curves, light values against dark, large-scale objects against small. Without the element of conflict, design is washed out and boring.

Repetition. A color, shape, or direction repeated in the display strengthens the impact of the whole. An example might be six identical mannequin heads, each wearing a hat of the same model in a different color, leaving no doubt about what item the store is promoting and the colors in which it is available.

Dominance. Whether it is the classification of merchandise or a new color or fabric, one overriding theme must be established in order to fortify the point being made.

Armed with good design principles, the visual-display designer proceeds to plan and stage the display. The materials with which the display is created can be almost anything the designer's imagination can summon, from common, mundane items to sophisticated mannequins.

MANNEQUINS

She is not someone you'd invite to your dinner party. It is not because she is 6 feet tall and beautiful, wears a perfect size 6, obviously works out at the gym, and doesn't know the meaning of "a bad hair day." It's just that she wouldn't add anything to the conversation.

Still, she is very good at her job—she sells more merchandise than any salesperson in the store where she works.

If she is employed by Saks Fifth Avenue, her name is Frannie, the first custom-made mannequin the store has ordered in 20 years. They say she is more than a pretty face and a perfect body. Reportedly she has the quality any mannequin would kill for. It is called "window appeal."

Frannie put Frances out of work. It seems that even though Frances is a cool beauty—modeled after Grace Kelly—she is too short (5 feet 8 inches) and a little too fleshy (size 8). Frances has the look of a lady who'd rather run to lunch than run the track, so she had to go.

Frances joins the parade of silent salespeople who no longer reflect the times. It is a matter of a constantly changing image for both men and women. In order to supply the "model" men and women who would wear next year's fashions, mannequin makers introduce new collections twice a year.

For instance, for almost 60 years the standard male mannequin had a 38-inch chest and a 32-inch waist. But working out in the gym has paid off. Now their chests have grown to 40 inches and their waists have been exercised down to 30 inches.

The faces of mannequins are often modeled after real-life beauties. Even the less famous are born through a complicated process. A sculptor uses real models to create a clay statue. A mold is made by casting the statue into plaster. While mannequins were once made of wax and wood, today's beauty is likely made of fiberglass. Makeup artists apply lashes and lip color. Hairstylists design perfect wigs.

The mannequin's joints are so perfectly articulated that they can assume any human position. Many have realistic hands. The finished mannequin costs about $800.

In addition to full-body forms, stores often use partial figures (busts or torsos), floppy stuffed muslin or soft sculpture figures, cutouts, and dressmaker forms. Avant-garde fashion stores often use abstract molded figures, hairless and featureless and tinted to match the background colors.

DEPARTMENT DISPLAY

Mannequins are one way of displaying merchandise. However, the merchandise items themselves can be exhibited as an exciting display, hung against walls or placed in such a way that they become design elements in themselves.

The merchandise that the customer sees upon entering a department has been purposefully arranged in or on *fixtures* in such a way that it attracts the eye. This is a vital aspect of visual merchandising, since it is where the sales are actually made.

"Fixturing" refers to free-standing floor units, wall projections, display cases, and bins and shelving, which hold the merchandise. They are constructed of wood, glass, Lucite, or chrome.

Fixtures are designed to provide neat and attractive display, allowing for ease of selection and decision making. Most are adjustable for rapid change in accommodating new assortments of merchandise as it arrives in the store.

The classification of merchandise dictates the kind of fixturing that will be used. Coordinates, for example, require floor racks on which they can be hung by color and fabric groupings. Folded sweaters make the greatest visual impact displayed in shelves or compartment bins.

Store image and the target customer also dictate the type of fixturing used. What works in the junior department is not appropriate for the designer salon.

The objective for the World Foot Locker store was high-volume turnovers. Both the store's design and its fixturing allow for the in-depth selection of styles and sizes to be displayed on the selling floor.

The creative fixture featured in Figure 13.2 not only moves the athletic shoes away from the traditional wall unit, it provides the feeling of movement while providing department definition. The shoes seemingly float on air. The plexiglass fixture is in keeping with the openness of the store's design, enabling the customer to see through into the next area. While the customer shops for a running shoe, he or she is subtly being sold fashion sports apparel at the same time.

The hat fixture, featured in Figure 13.3, is a stroke of genius in fixturing design. You will note in Figure 13.1 that the fixture is tall enough to be seen from outside the store. Acting as a visual anchor toward the rear of the store, it projects

Figure 13.2
The plexiglass fixtures are in keeping with the open design of the store and provide the customer with an unobstructed view of other merchandise. Courtesy of the Athletic Specialty Division of Woolworth Corporation.

depth of selection and choice. Its circular shape serves to draw the customer around, exposing the customer to the rest of the merchandise offered in the store. From the practical standpoint, it is cleverly designed to store the backstock of this item.

Valuable impulse sales are made via point-of-sale installations (sometimes referred to as point-of-purchase, or POP). Prime examples are in supermarkets, mass marketers, or discounters where racks of candy, magazines, batteries, cigarette lighters, and myriad other small necessities are displayed at the check-out counters, with the maker's name prominently displayed alongside or on the display unit.

In the sophisticated department and specialty stores, the presentation is more subtle, but the purpose is the same. The shopper may find small racks of merchandise set on display cases related to the department classification. For example, in the blouse section, racks might hold accessories like silk ties. In active wear, baskets filled with bright terry stretch headbands or sport socks would stimulate multiple sales at the point of purchase.

Figure 13.3

The hat fixture is visible from outside the store; it performs both functional and visual merchandising duties. Courtesy of the Athletic Specialty Division of Woolworth Corporation.

SIGNS

By now you may have noticed that no signs were used at the World Foot Locker except for the store's logo. Few retailers have the openness of this store. For most merchants, signs are an important form of communication with the customer, as well as a powerful method of in-store advertising.

Signing delivers information while conveying the image of the store. The graphics of the signs must blend with the store's interior and exterior design. Above all, signs must be attractive and useful to the viewer.

Signing refers to all printed wording that carries the store's message to the customer and is embodied in all manner of shapes and forms, simple and elaborate.

On the face of the building exterior is the store's signature, or logo, stylized to establish an identity. The same signature will be seen in reduced version on boxes, bags, store stationery, and business cards.

In windows, signs reinforce a merchandising thrust in just a few well-chosen words—a designer's name, a slogan that has been widely used in store advertising, or a phrase that furthers the theme of the window.

Permanent signs within the store identify shops that carry a particular classification of merchandise or feature a particular designer or manufacturer, such as "Izod" or "Ralph Lauren."

Printed wall signs, free-standing signboards, and countertop signs announce special events, sales, or store services.

In creating a sign, the designer thinks about content, graphic design, and positioning.

Content.   The fewer words used to get the message across the better. A sign's language is composed with as much care as good advertising copy, clearly stated, and edited down to its essence so that the shopper can absorb it in a short period of time.

Design.   The graphic design of a sign refers to its lettering style, color, and the material of which it is constructed. The final product must be suitable to the area in which it is placed. For example, permanent signing for a children's department could be lowercase block letters carved of wood, painted in primary red, yellow, and blue, and affixed to a prominent wall. The people who craft and letter signs are attuned to the nuances of typeface and color. Input comes from the fashion director or visual-display director to ensure that current trends are reflected and that some semblance of conformity is maintained throughout the store.

Positioning.   Signs are posted taking into account traffic patterns in the store, considering where customers are most likely to pause.

Both lettered and constructed signs are created in the sign shops of large stores. Smaller operations without the means to produce signs in-store must seek independent sign-makers.

LIGHTING

Good lighting is crucial to display. Too bright, and there is a garish glare: the lighting competes with the merchandise; not bright enough, and the display fades into the background.

A variety of lighting techniques are used to highlight a display: floodlights at the base of the display, track lighting overhead, or even a strobe or colored lights.

The Visual Merchandising Team

The visual merchandiser is an artist, designer, architectural whiz, and space planner who coordinates the creative efforts of the display staff. The size of the staff may range from a single person to an army of 20 or more in a large store.

When there is a large corps, labor is divided between technically skilled designers, painters, artists, carpenters, electricians, sign-makers, and store-planning draftspeople. The single display person has to be a jack-of-all-trades, performing all the necessary jobs to pull the display together. In some cases, the owner-operator adds display to the roles performed.

At the top of the managerial pyramid of a large store, the visual merchandiser or display director (there are several appropriate titles) oversees managers of divisions, which may be divided by function, such as windows and interior display, or by merchandise classification, such as fashion and hard goods.

Display responsibility is divided by merchandise when the store is too large for one team to handle the work involved. Display people in each area are acquainted with the merchandise and are able to show it to the best advantage.

While display people are some of the most creative to be found in the store, they are rarely in direct contact with the fashion market and must rely on information from the buyers and fashion director. Far in advance of the season, the fashion office schedules which department will be featured in windows, and when. The schedule often includes a trend report to cue the display staff of the fashion direction on the horizon.

Suppose that you are a sportswear buyer for a large department store. It is June, and your vendors are beginning to ship fall orders. Your department is still in summer, but by the end of July, displays will be in fall gear, and fall merchandise will be displayed up front while summer clearance merchandise is fixtured at the rear of the department.

First, you and the fashion office must decide which items will be displayed. Selections will be based on (1) items that best express current fashion trends and (2) items for which there will be plenty of backup stock.

Detailed information on the items for display is gathered and submitted via a printed form to the display department. The form will list the following: names of vendors, style and department numbers, classification (what the merchandise is—skirt, jacket, sweater), a brief description of each item, the color story, recommendations as to signing, when the merchandise will be available to the visual merchandising team, and delivery dates for the bulk of the merchandise ordered.

In some cases, you and the display staff will meet for discussion to clarify fashion trends.

The display staff takes it from there, sketching, planning, sharing their ideas, constructing and collecting props and mannequins, and collecting the merchandise.

When actual construction begins, the visual merchandising director coordinates the work and supervises its installation. In the final display, mannequins are dressed and accessorized according to the dictates of the fashion office and department buyer.

The success of the display is measured in the sales that result. A sellout of the merchandise displayed proves that the display effectively promoted the item.

Summary

Visual merchandising reinforces the sell-through of goods in the store. Window displays attract the customer into the store, while interior displays provide sales stimuli inside the store. Windows are often highly creative theaters of fashion. Interior displays are designed to blend with architectural elements and the floor plan of the store while exciting the interest of the prospective customer.

Visual merchandising employs basic design principles, working with various materials and colors. While mannequins are often used, the merchandise itself is often equally effective as a display. Interior display combines fixtures, lighting effects, and signs to feature and promote the merchandise.

The display team works closely with buyers and the fashion director, who select the merchandise and supply fashion information. The success of a display effort is measured by sales that result.

Terms for Review

1. Exterior display
2. Interior display
3. Closed-back windows
4. Open-back windows
5. Partially open windows

6. Shadow-box windows
7. Island windows
8. Adjacencies
9. Fixtures

Study Review Questions

1. What does visual merchandising accomplish for the retailer?
2. How do displays provide guidance?
3. What is the objective of window display?
4. Explain the concept of adjacencies.
5. Name and describe the principles of display.
6. How do store image and merchandise affect the choice of fixtures?
7. Describe why signs are important to the retailer.

Case

Take a field trip and "shop" three stores. If possible, try to visit stores that target different customers, for example, a high-end fashion store, a store that is moderately priced and geared to the junior customer, and a department store.

Questions

1. Compare the three stores' use of window displays, noting the type of window, what made the display effective, and whether the store's target customer could be determined by the display.
2. Compare the three stores in terms of the interior visual merchandising, including interior design, fixturing, and displays.
3. Compare the three stores in terms of the signs used. Comment on the effectiveness of the signs and the message communicated.

14 SPECIAL EVENTS

Another important facet of sales promotion is the *special event*. While some special-event activities are directly intended to promote selling, many of the special events a retailer offers are intended to do much more than move merchandise. By providing entertainment, enlightenment, and social services, the store is positioning itself as a community center—a place to go whether or not there is a need to purchase goods.

The retailer is part of the basic fabric of a community. Just as a city or town derives its identity from its industries, clubs, restaurants, theaters, museums, and parks, the retailer too adds an important dimension to the community. Through the special events it offers, a store is able to express its interest in and commitment to the community. Special events that involve the store in the social and civic life of the community build goodwill and demonstrate that the store sees itself as more than a business.

Special events also afford an opportunity for the store to establish an identity and personality different from its competition. The showmanship, excitement, and educational value delivered through special events add an important dimension to the store's image.

Ultimately special events accomplish what all sales promotion activities are intended to do: draw customers into the store and move merchandise out. While the event itself may not be tied to merchandise, it increases customer traffic. By bringing numbers of people into the store, the special event exposes people to the merchandise the store has to offer. It also helps people to form the habit of visiting the store. In theory, the special event the store presents today will increase sales in the future.

The shopping habit is an important factor to retailers. It is estimated that 60% of all retail sales are made in the first store the customer enters. Through the special event, the retailer tries to establish itself as that "first" store. The special event is used as a means of establishing a strong, positive impression of the store in the customer's mind.

Types of Special Events

It is difficult to clearly define a special event by type—most are a creative combination. The institutional event does, eventually, result in merchandise sales, and the promotional event should always be institutional insofar as it promotes the image of the store.

Even the individual event is hard to classify. Here too, the event will often combine elements from past successes. Rarely is there something new or never tried; the excitement of a special event is the way the retailer borrows, adapts, and molds the idea to make the event uniquely its own. Part of the challenge of special-event planning is to give the illusion that it is happening for the very first time.

The word "tie-in" is common to the discussion of special events. Possibilities for tie-ins are limited only by the level of creativity and resourcefulness of event planning—and, of course, by store image and target customer. Tie-ins afford the retailer the opportunity to increase the excitement of the event; they also help stretch the sales promotion budget if associated costs are shared.

INSTITUTIONAL SPECIAL EVENTS

Some special events are institutional in nature, in that they are not designed to prompt an immediate sale of merchandise. It is important to remember, however, that even *institutional special events* sell, since they "sell" the image the store wishes to project to the public.

The institutional special event wins goodwill and often attracts people into the store. There are instances when the store conducts off-site special events. Such store-sponsored events as parades, marathons, or athletic events serve to establish the store as part of the community and get the store talked or written about.

Macy's Thanksgiving Day Parade is perhaps the best known annual, off-site special event. Symbolizing the kickoff of the Christmas holiday shopping season, the parade, featured in Figure 14.1, delights some 80 million people on a day when the store is closed. This institutional special event has itself become an institution in the New York City community and, through TV coverage, throughout the country—so much, in fact, that Judge Burton R. Lifland made the continuation of the Macy's Thanksgiving Day Parade a condition for the approval of the merger between R. H. Macy and Federated Department Stores.

Retailer-sponsored black-tie dinners is another example of an institutional special event. Invitations are sent to the community's elite, and the proceeds from the event are donated to a worthy cause or organization. Philanthropic motives

Figure 14.1

Macy's Thanksgiving Day Parade kicks off the holiday selling season with goodwill for the store. Courtesy of Macy's.

notwithstanding, the store usually garnishes plenty of positive publicity from such an event.

Stores often sponsor educational seminars or classes in the store or at an off-site location. The event that makes experts available to the public is perceived as providing a valued service. This type of event, especially when held in the store, also serves to introduce new customers to the store.

The topics of these special events are limitless; anything that would interest or enlighten the store's customers is appropriate. Exercise classes, tips on gardening, dealing with the problems of child-rearing, and how to get back into the job market are just a few examples of the topics covered in store-sponsored classes.

Exhibits are another form of institutional special event. Often the exhibit is a result of a tie-in with another major institution in the community, such as the museum or the public library. Stores also use exhibits to acknowledge community groups like the Boy Scouts, Girl Scouts, or volunteer firefighters.

Local or national events, such as the space program or a community's centennial celebration, provide themes for store exhibits. Science exhibits or displays of antiques or costumes may be used simply to draw people into the store.

MERCHANDISE-RELATED SPECIAL EVENTS

Some special events are designed to directly increase the store's sales. The *merchandise-related special event* is directly tied to merchandise the store carries.

Demonstrations, for example, are particularly helpful in moving merchandise since people are persuaded to purchase a product by seeing it in action. In-store demonstrations are often free to the retailer—the manufacturer supplies the personnel and foots the bill. New appliances for food preparation are commonly introduced to the public through demonstrations, as are new products in the cosmetic department.

The special event advertised in Figure 14.2 has a foot in both the institutional and promotional camps. The ad says that the executive chef of the Westin Hotel will be at the store demonstrating how to prepare a number of mouth-watering recipes. While the event appears to be institutional, consider this: as Chef Wade works his magic, he will use the tools of the trade that the store sells.

The event also appears cooperative. The Westin Hotel name is prominent in the ad; the additional enticement of the event—a weekend at a Westin hotel—

Figure 14.2

Shillito's draws the customer in by offering demonstrations of recipe preparation, but features its merchandise in the process. Notice the tie-in with the Westin Hotel. Courtesy of *Retail Ad Week* magazine.

indicates that both Shillito's and the Westin hotel chain shared in the increased exposure and expense of the event.

Holiday or seasonal events are a popular draw. The challenge is to add a dimension of newness and excitement. Visits to the store by the Easter bunny or the most famous North Pole resident have been done to death; the store must creatively add a new angle to stand out from the competition.

Celebrity appearances and personal appearances are often tied into merchandise offered in the store. The designer personal appearance, for instance, is an important selling incentive in the store's fashion departments. Customers are drawn to the store due to curiosity or because the designer has an aura of authority. Autograph sessions with book authors or with movie stars and sports figures who have endorsed merchandise are further examples of the merchandise-related special event.

Again, the event does not have to be directly tied to merchandise to be an effective means to introduce customers to the store's selection. Nordstrom ran a series of special events during its opening of a new store at The Westchester, a mall in White Plains, New York. One of the events extended an invitation to the general public to join Greg Gumbel, the sports personality, in The Pub for a buffet dinner. (The Pub is just one of the conveniences the store offers; the store also boasts a concierge, two restaurants, a package and coat check, and an espresso bar.)

Co-hosted by American Express, the event included a sports trivia contest, a review of whiskeys and cigars by *Cigar Afficionado* magazine, and parting gifts. Participants were charged $25, and an R.S.V.P. was required. Finally, the gathering adjourned to a shop within the store, where participates were given a chance to meet Greg Gumbel personally.

Through this event, the store not only introduced participants to The Pub, but also to the interior of the store. Further, since the store opening coincided with the opening of the mall itself, the event also served to sow the seed of the shopping habit.

Products inspired by the popularity of a movie or TV show are often promoted by special tie-in events; personal appearances, free posters or tee-shirts, tickets to the filming or premier showing, and trip raffles typify this kind of special event.

Sleep shirts inspired by the popularity of daytime soaps were a natural for a special event that featured guest appearances by two soap opera stars, as advertised in the Hess's ad in Figure 14.3.

THE FASHION EVENT

There are many variations on the *fashion event,* each serving to accomplish a different goal.

As previously mentioned, the personal appearance of the designer is effective in bringing customers into the store. The event featuring the designer appearance can be as simple as the designer being available in the department to meet

Figure 14.3

Hess's capitalizes on a special-events natural: guest appearances by soap stars to promote sleep shirts with that theme. Notice the clever copy. Courtesy of *Retail Ad Week* magazine.

customers and answer questions or make suggestions. Informal modeling is often added to aid the buying impulse.

Other dimensions are sometimes added to the designer personal appearance. Continental breakfasts or coffee and dessert may be served, depending of the time of day the event is scheduled.

A single designer runway show is the next level of a fashion event tie-in with the designer personal appearance. This type of event is appropriate for the store that has made a considerable investment in the designer's collection.

The *trunk show* is another type of fashion event used by retailers. The trunk show serves several purposes. Since this type of event involves presenting merchandise from the line that is not available at the store, either because the store has not purchased the merchandise or because the items are from the next season, all the participants benefit. The manufacturer is given an opportunity to completely showcase the full line, directly interact with the ultimate customer, and take special orders. The trunk show then yields the store goodwill from both the customer and the supplier.

The trunk show enables the retailer to take a reading on customer interest. Special orders for next season's merchandise, for instance, act as a barometer for the store, helping the store to focus its orders. Further, the trunk show is a low-risk, high-gain proposition for the store. With this type of fashion event, the store plays liaison between customer and manufacturer without having to invest in the merchandise. Finally, the trunk show helps to establish a fashion headquarters image for the store.

Fashion events that involve tie-ins with magazines take numerous forms, from the simple informative seminar to a full-blown runway fashion show. The store gains from the association with the magazine, whose editors are perceived to have fashion credentials. The fashion event built upon a magazine tie-in acts as a third-party endorsement of the store and its fashion selection, while increasing traffic and merchandise sales.

The fashion event is oftentimes structured to position the retailer as the arbitrator of fashion. From informal modeling to the full-fledged runway show, retailers use this type of fashion event to educate its customers on how to assemble the newest looks and to promote its image as a fashion headquarters.

Informal modeling yields impact without requiring much in the way of planning and expense. "Fashion shows" on a smaller scale, informal modeling conducted within the department, throughout the store, or in select areas, such as the store's restaurant during the lunch service, serve to expose the customer to fashion trends and available merchandise.

Similarly, informal modeling provides a less expensive vehicle for the store to reach its target customer off-site. Cooperation with appropriate organizations and groups provide the opportunity; the retailer provides the models and merchandise at the off-site location where the store's target customers have assembled, such as a women's group luncheon.

The premier showcase for the store's fashion merchandise is the full-fledged fashion show. With professional models, music, scenery, and commentary, the fashion show dramatically introduces the new season's fashion trends and merchandise. If it is co-sponsored with a local institution or structured as a fund-raising event, the fashion show is an opportunity for the store to win institutional goodwill and new potential customers.

Such a show is often staged in a large area: the store's auditorium, its restaurant, or an area cleared of merchandise for the event. It also could be held outside the store, in a designated area of the shopping mall, in a rented facility, or at the site of a co-sponsoring organization.

THE STOREWIDE EVENT

While the types of events discussed so far would involve the "entire store" in the case of a small retailer, the large retail store could conceivably be conducted several unrelated events simultaneously since the "target customer" would be different for each event. While the event in a specific department helps the entire store in that it serves to build traffic and establish image, the goals of the event, and its measured results, are narrow.

The storewide event is different in that it is a united total store event. It is commonly built around store news—such as an anniversary or new branch opening, a holiday, or community event.

Major retailers have taken the various types of special events and expanded them into a storewide, multiweek extravaganza. Built upon a central theme, the *storewide event* features specially purchased merchandise, multidepartment involvement, and the full complement of sales promotion support. The theme is promoted through the use of shopping bags designed for the occasion, store ads, window displays, and "special" special events that are planned and executed throughout the store.

Months, sometimes years in the planning, storewide events mean huge traffic and retail sales for the store. Bloomingdale's, famous for its ambitious storewide promotions, estimated that "Fete de France" drew 2 to 3 million people into its Manhattan headquarters alone, and the number of people attracted to its 14 units during the seven-week event totaled 12 million.

Black-tie galas are commonly used to kick off the storewide event. The store generates goodwill and plenty of press by inviting prominent figures from politics, society, and the fashion world to the store for a formal dinner to benefit a charity, a local institution or cause, or the arts. Then, throughout the duration of the storewide event, the store's individual departments are alive with activity—enticing people in.

Key to Success

For a special event to be effective, it must be of interest to the audience it is intended to attract. In other words, a seminar on gardening is not likely to draw large crowds to the junior department.

What constitutes a successful special event, therefore, changes with the times. There are, of course, perennial winners, those events that annually draw people to the store and become a vital aspect of the store's image. However, the competitiveness of the retail environment heightens the demand for creativity in special events.

To be successful, the store must have a finger on the pulse of society and have a sense for the events that will entice its customers in. Special events based on what is topical will draw the largest crowds.

Figure 14.4

Special events lend excitement to shopping, giving the customer a reason to come into the store. Courtesy of *Retail Ad Week* magazine.

Responsibility for Special Events

Everyone in the retail store, from buyer to sales promotion director, has a hand in special events.

Buyers often think of events that would help sell the merchandise in their departments. They are, after all, in tune with what concerns their customers and often know what event will draw them into the store. In addition, buyers hear of special-event opportunities from their resources.

Merchandise managers are often responsible for theme events in their departments. They look for events that will help their areas reach the sales goals that have been set. Upper management takes an even larger view of special events—searching for ways to reinforce the store's image and position in the market.

But the responsibility for execution falls on the shoulders of the special-events department. It is here that the loose ends are tied together. It takes tremendous coordination within the retail store to execute a special event.

The special-events department oversees the entire process, from ordering napkins for the seminar luncheon to ensuring that the proper advertising and display support are in place.

Summary

The many, varied activities a store offers the public add excitement, showmanship, and drama to the shopping experience. Special events serve to connect the store with the community, building goodwill and encouraging patronage. Through its special events, a store communicates and differentiates its image to the general public and to its customers.

Terms for Review

1. Special event
2. Institutional special event
3. Merchandise-related special event
4. Fashion event
5. Trunk show
6. Storewide event

Study Review Questions

1. Why do retailers use special events?
2. How do special events enable the store to express its interest in and commitment to the community?
3. Compare the institutional special event with the merchandise-related event.

4. Who was the target customer for the Greg Gumbel personal appearance event at Nordstrom's?

5. Name two different forms of the fashion event and what they accomplish for the retailer.

Case

Choose any retailer with which you are familiar and plan a special event. Outline the main objective of the event and provide details of the event itself. Since you are the "special-events staff," it is your responsibility to attend to every detail required to make the event a success.

Questions

1. How the event will be advertised; what media mix should be used to best reach the target audience for the event?

2. How long in advance of the event—by weeks—did it take you to fully pull the event together?

3. How can the success of the event be measured?

15

PUBLICITY: A Different Drummer

"…The fashion industry as a whole is the most promotion-minded of all industries. Wholesalers, designers, manufacturers, retailers, department store buyers—each is alert to the possibilities of pre-selling their product. And well they must be. Geared to fashion deadlines and operating in a field where competitors' throats are cut with as much finesse as an evening gown, they cannot wait for customers to discover them—they must cry their wares in the marketplace."[1]

Around the turn of the century on Manhattan's Lower East Side, small store owners would go to almost any length to get a customer into the store. A common method was to take up a position outside the store and harangue passersby, literally blocking their way, if necessary, while employing a complicated series of gestures and fast talk guaranteed to stop the potential customer in his or her tracks.

It is still nostalgically recalled in retailing circles that some of these salesmen used a cane, which they would hook deftly into the pocket of a man's suit or around his arm in order to physically draw the customer into the store, where they could continue their "spiel" to make the sale. It was a hard way to sell, but it often worked.

Meanwhile, the competition uptown was using the velvet touch on its carriage trade. Horse-drawn cabs would deliver customers to the grand entrance of the store, where a liveried doorman would usher them inside. After they were comfortably seated in the department, a bevy of deferential salesgirls would cater to their every whim. Service was the watchword.

[1]Constance Hope, *Publicity Is Broccoli* (New York: Bobbs-Merrill, 1941).

While some of the so-called better stores had begun to advertise in local papers and national magazines, much of their reputation was built by word of mouth.

We've come a long way since then. Today, we recognize that the powerful sell of paid media exposure is what produces profits. However, there is another kind of exposure that is equally vital: *publicity*.

The function of publicity is to keep the store's name on the lips of the public. Most large department stores maintain publicity departments as an arm of public relations. But the small retailer need not miss out on the opportunities publicity affords. In this chapter, we will examine what publicity is, what it accomplishes, and how to successfully conduct publicity.

WHAT IS PUBLICITY?

Publicity, plainly put, is news. It is distinct from advertising in both its purpose and function. Advertising is paid for, publicity is not. Publicity is not public relations; rather, it is an extension of public relations.

Publicity seeks to present the store as a solid citizen in the community. It does so through coverage of events that are of interest to the public. It stimulates the interest of the news media (newspapers, radio, TV, magazines) by communicating the store's newsworthy events to the editors and programmers who prepare the news for public consumption. It is then up to the discretion of the media whether or not to use the information reported. There is no guarantee that the editors will make use of the store's publicity or, in the event it is accepted, that the news will be favorably presented.

To get store publicity placed, it is necessary to understand the needs of the markets to which the news is directed. The editor's purpose is to interest the reader; the program director's aim is to interest the viewer or listener. Therefore, these decision makers will accept only news that is pertinent to their audience segment. Material must also be appropriate to the overall editorial content of the publication. For example, the announcement of a new store president might be sent to the business editors of the local papers and perhaps to the editors of the business magazines and retail trade publications. A celebrity appearance tied in with a new film and related products to be sold in the store might be of interest to editors of newspaper Style sections and to local TV stations.

In the event that an editor accepts a news item from the publicist, the story may be run simply as a mention in a column, or it may receive lengthier treatment as a *news story* or a *feature story*. A news story is one which presents the straight, unvarnished facts of an event, written in condensed form. The feature story contains all the facts, but within a more entertaining format. The difference is also in organization. While the straight news story contains all the facts in the first paragraph, the feature allows the facts to be revealed within the second or third paragraph. The publicist might submit a story to an editor written in either news or feature form, based on an understanding of the editor's requirements.

How Publicity Differs from "PR" and Advertising

An advertising message, such as a full-page newsprint ad or a manufacturer's ad in a national fashion magazine, is controlled by the advertiser. It is paid for, produced, and placed for the ultimate purpose of producing sales.

Generally, an advertisement must meet the standards of the publication in which it is to appear. A magazine of the caliber of *Vogue*, for example, prides itself on excellent design. The typography, photography, and artwork of the editorial portion of the *book,* as a magazine is called, are a matter of honor. The visual image establishes a magazine's image just as surely as a store's fashion assortment and decor establish its image.

Responsible publishers will refuse to compromise fine design with advertisements that do not live up to their standards, even though refusing a tasteless or poorly designed ad will mean lost revenue.

"Public relations" is a term often used synonymously with "publicity." Although in some cases their functions overlap, they are not the same thing.

Public relations strives to establish and maintain a favorable store image in the eyes of the public—its vendors, customers, investors, and others who may have direct contact with the store. It does so through a preplanned, long-range program, with goodwill for the store as its objective. Conversely, publicity is usually a short-range affair, owing to the nature of fast-breaking news and the need for timeliness.

Here's how its works: As a part of its public relations program, let us say that Lord & Taylor decides to run free career clinics for women during the same week that the store is introducing a new Career Clothing boutique. The "plan" of the public relations campaign is to project Lord & Taylor as an organization concerned about its customers—in this case, the woman who is the target customer of the Career Clothing boutique.

Among the speakers to appear at the clinics are celebrated experts in their own fields, well known to the press and the public. Prior to the events, the advertising department prepares newsprint ads announcing the new department, along with a calendar of the free career clinics and related store promotions.

The publicity department sends *press releases* to its list of newspaper and magazine editors and radio and TV programmers, along with invitations to attend a kick-off dinner hosted by the store. The $100-a-plate dinner will be attended by the city's social elite. The proceeds from the dinner, planned by public relations and executed by special events, will benefit New Start, a nonprofit organization formed to help underprivileged women train for and find career jobs.

As a follow-up, publicity will send *press kits* containing captioned photographs of the speakers and copies of news releases to all editors who could not attend the week-long event and possibly to those who did.

The desired outcome: the story is picked up in the Style section of *The New York Times* and the Living section of a suburban newspaper chain. Three network TV channels feature the dinner event, which they have videotaped for the late evening news. The next morning, a network news show features a clip of the famous arriving at the benefit dinner as an introduction to a segment on New Start. The director of the organization is interviewed, and the store receives mention again, for the benefit it has sponsored and the career clinics it is offering. Later in the week, a phone-in radio show has as its guest one of the clinic speakers. Again, the store receives mention throughout the program.

The end result: the store is perceived as a responsible institution with an interest in public affairs as well as a store with fashion sense. The public opinion of it is raised. The dynamics of advertising, public relations, special events, and publicity have operated to complement one another to the fullest capacity.

This is, of course, an idealized situation. Not all publicity efforts enjoy this level of success.

The Role of the Fashion Publicist

The publicist must be adept at perceiving newsworthy events the moment they occur. Equally important is the ability to create news to attract media attention. The publicist needs a well-developed imagination, persuasive powers, writing and verbal skills, and an ability to work as a team member. In addition, the publicist requires a thick skin in order to withstand the rejections that will often come from editors.

The publicist's daily schedule is charged with details and pressures. To do the job properly the publicist must:

- Hold press conferences
- Discuss and promote fashion items with the editors
- Research and write facts of interest about the store
- Gather data and maintain detailed source lists and files
- Write press releases and prepare press kits
- Plan publicity campaigns
- Direct photography sessions
- Communicate verbally with industry and store personnel

Since it is necessary for the publicist to establish a network of media and industry contacts, a source list must be maintained and regularly updated. The outline for such a list might look like this:

Editors

- Consumer magazines
- Trade magazines and journals
- Newspapers, city and local
- Syndicates
- Wire services

Program directors, producers

- Local TV and radio stations of national affiliates
- National news and magazine-format shows
- Local news and magazine-format shows
- Conversation and debate shows
- Cable TV stations

Industry

- Manufacturers (fashion coordinators)
- Trade organizations
- Licensing companies
- Designers

In-store

- Buyers
- Fashion director
- Special-events coordinator
- Decision makers

The publicist receives support and ideas from the store's buyers, fashion coordinators, and other executives in the store. Fashion coordinators, for example, will seek publicity support to introduce a fashion to the customer before the merchandise reaches the selling floor. Working together, the fashion coordinator and publicist will seek ways to get the "news" into the media.

Reporting the Store's News

To develop a compelling news story out of an event, the publicist first seeks an "angle," the slant on the news that would appeal to the medium targeted. To be successful, the publicist must have a clear idea of what editors (program directors) and their readers (viewers) want. To do this, the publicist needs to know and understand the target audience of the medium that the press release will be sent to. Armed with this knowledge, the publicist presents the store's news with an angle that will interest a particular medium. In some cases this requires several "versions" of the press release on the same news item, each with a slightly different slant.

Sources of interesting news can be found throughout the store, under the heading of store business, fashion trends, special events, or outstanding individuals. The following are some activities that often provide news themes for publicity:

- Major renovations
- New products
- Branch store openings
- New department concepts

- New designer affiliations
- Special customer services
- Public service events
- Fashion shows
- Storewide promotions
- Free seminars
- Personnel changes
- New credit policies
- Celebrity appearances
- Financial news

This list is by no means all inclusive. Creativity is the mark of a successful publicity effort. Having a "finger-on-the-pulse" comes in a close second. The publicist is always looking for ways to create news for the store. Knowing what is current and topical is crucial—if the reader (viewer) will be interested, so will the editor (program director).

In developing news themes, the publicist will often meet with executives, merchandise managers, and buyers to collect information and develop half-formed ideas into well-organized stories.

Finally, the news is delivered to the media in the form of a press release. The release should contain all the information an editor or programmer will need to construct a story suitable to the vehicle. The individual editor decides how to use the information particular to his or her needs and the needs of that vehicle's audience.

News releases are welcomed by most publications and the electronic media. In fact, many newspapers and magazines rely heavily on press releases to fill their pages. It has been estimated that approximately one quarter of the editorial matter in daily newspapers comes from releases that have been submitted by publicity people.

The "story" may be a result of the editor or producer using the material as submitted. Other times, the information in the press release in used in part or is included in a story with other information. The "home run" for the publicist is when the press release perks enough interest that the editor or producer uses it as a starting point for further investigation. In this case, the editor or producer gets in touch with the publicist and makes further inquiries; the resulting story or program features the store and the news about it.

Elements of a Good Press Release

There are general rules to consider when writing a press release; in addition, there is an accepted format for press releases, in style, format, and content. For the press release to be successful, that is, to generate publicity for the retailer, both the general rules and the accepted format must be followed.

Figure 15.1 is the three-page press release for Neiman Marcus's 1994 Christmas Book. In this section we will examine both the general and specifics of writing and placing publicity releases for the retailer, using the Neiman Marcus press release as a guide.

Media Information

FOR IMMEDIATE RELEASE
Monday, Sept. 12, 1994

CONTACT:
Jodie Pogue, Liz Barrett, Carolyn Cobb
Neiman Marcus
1618 Main Street
Dallas, Texas 75201
214/573-5778, 5783, 5622

NEIMAN MARCUS UNVEILS 1994 CHRISTMAS BOOK

DALLAS -- Neiman Marcus today unwrapped the earliest gift of the 1994 holiday season, releasing its famous Christmas Book and announcing the much-heralded "His and Hers" gift.

An aquatic adventurer's fantasy, this year's "His and Hers" gift promises to revolutionize the scuba industry. The Bellaqua **Breathing Observation Bubble, known as BOB**, is a portable, battery-driven diving "scooter" in which one can cruise quietly underwater at depths of up to 40 feet. BOB transports its passenger through the water in an upright, seated position with an attached Plexiglas bubble dome supplying a constant airflow around the rider's head and shoulders. Priced at $7,500, BOB can be equipped with an optional built-in communication system for use between BOBs for $1,500. *Page 116.*

For those who prefer to stay afloat, Neiman Marcus offers a whisper-quiet **Electric Gondola** for two. Powered by a rechargeable motor, the $7,400 craft features a built-in ice bucket, removable cassette player and wooden canopy with curtain. *Page 91.*

For those shopping for more conventional gifts, the Christmas Book features a variety of men's and women's apparel, jewelry, leather goods, children's wear and toys, in a wide range of prices.

Neiman Marcus   -more-

Figure 15.1

This three-page press release announced the unveiling of the Neiman Marcus 1994 Christmas Book. Courtesy of Neiman Marcus.

add one – Neiman Marcus 1994 Christmas Book

Returning this year: "Things You Didn't Know You Needed," an eclectic array of gifts including a life-size "Skeleton in Your Closet" sachet and "A Bird in the Hand" gardening gloves. And, back by popular demand are the "$25 and Under" pages.

If the family goldfish are in the market for larger living quarters, Neiman Marcus offers a 10-foot-tall **Elephant-Shaped Aquarium** for $120,000. The 300-gallon tank is made of hand-carved, polished acrylic and rests atop a pedestal base that houses the aquarium's inner electrical workings. *Page 23.*

Animal lovers can put more than a new puppy under the tree with a pet that is great for kids and adults alike: **Miniature Donkeys**. Only 29 to 38 inches tall, these small wonders are completely domesticated, extremely affectionate, and are available for $1,300 to $7,000, depending on gender, color and pedigree. *Page 5.*

Dream about a white Christmas in a **Russian Imperial Sleigh Bed** designed by Rhett Judice. The queen-sized bed features gold-leaf detailing, hand-painted troika designs and comes with a velvet bedspread and pillows. Priced at $18,000, it is crowned by a six-foot headboard with oval medallion for your monogram. *Page 90.*

For those who appreciate exquisite craftsmanship and the age-old tradition of fine tobacco, Neiman Marcus offers an exclusive **Humidor designed by Viscount David Linley.** Inspired by British architect Christopher Wren, who reconstructed London after the Great Fire, the large humidor is $14,000; a smaller version is $1,950. And to fill the humidor, there is a box of 25 cigars from the Dominican Republic for $90. *Page 60.*

-more-

Neiman Marcus

Figure 15.1

Continued

add two – Neiman Marcus 1994 Christmas Book

The Christmas Book's most precious jewel offering is an exquisite **18-karat gold Westminster Teddy Bear** holding a quartz pocket watch. British jewelry designer Jonathan Ralston labored for over 850 hours to create this masterpiece studded with 20 emeralds, 36 rubies, five carats of sapphires and 200 diamonds. The price: $200,000.

Page 61.

For the adventurous traveler: **"NM's First Tango,"** a seven-day trip to Buenos Aires, Argentina (Dec. 27, 1994–Jan. 2, 1995) for $5,995 per person, double occupancy. An optional six-day excursion to the pristine wilderness of Patagonia is offered for an additional sum. *Page 22.*

"Neiman Marcus has once again come up with a whimsical and unique collection of gifts, in keeping with our tradition of offering our customers the distinctive and the unusual," said Burt Tansky, Neiman Marcus chairman and CEO. "The Christmas Book really does have something for everyone," he added.

The cover of the 1994 Christmas Book was created by San Jose artist Mercedes McDonald. A portion of the proceeds from the sale of items depicting the Christmas Book cover art benefits the National Wildflower Research Center, founded by Lady Bird Johnson. The NWRC is committed to the preservation of North America's native flora.

This year's Christmas Book was introduced by Neiman Marcus today at the Loews Anatole Hotel in Dallas. The Christmas Book will be distributed to more than 3 million Neiman Marcus customers worldwide. To inquire about Christmas Book merchandise or to place an order, call 1-800-825-8781.

###

Neiman Marcus

Figure 15.1
Continued

GENERAL CONSIDERATIONS

- *A press release must be news.* When the press release lands on the editor's or program director's desk, it must be "news" to have perceived value. News can take the form of something different or unusual, or it can be based on timeliness—something that qualifies as news because it is currently on the public's mind.
- *Deadlines must be respected.* Each of the various media has a deadline. Consumer magazines, for example, are finalized long before they actually appear on the newsstand; the deadline for seasonal material can be as long as six months before the publication date. A publicist must know and respect the deadlines for the various media.
- *A "Contact" must be accessible.* The recipient must know who to contact regarding the press release, and that person, or persons, must be available to answer questions and supply additional information.

We will now look at Figure 15.1 to evaluate these general considerations.

News.   A retailer unveiling a Christmas catalog is not "news"; it is an annual and common event in the retailing industry. The news here is what is offered in the catalog. Neiman Marcus enjoys the reputation of offering exotic and expensive gifts through the store's Christmas catalog, and each year publicity is generated for the store by those gifts.

Deadline.   At the top left of Figure 15.1 is the *release date* of the press release.

While we are now concentrating on general considerations, the release date is an important aspect of format. Positioned at the top of the release, the release date tells the editor or program director when the information in the release can be used. Sometimes the topic of the press release would necessitate that the information should not be used *until* a certain date: "For release February 11." The press release is giving the editor advance notice of the news, but requesting that it not be made public until February 11.

Going back to the general consideration of deadline, the release date in the Neiman Marcus example has two parts. It is "FOR IMMEDIATE RELEASE," which means that the recipient can use the information as soon as it is received. The press release also carries an issue date: "Monday, Sept. 12, 1994." This press release was timed to give the editor or program director plenty of time to use the information.

Contact.   You will note at the top right of the release in Figure 15.1 that three people are listed, followed by the address of the store's corporate office and three corresponding telephone numbers where these contacts can be reached. Neiman Marcus ensures that it is accessible to answer any further questions regarding the content of the press release or to work with the editor or program director if expanded coverage is desired.

FORMAT CONSIDERATIONS

As previously stated, there is an accepted format for the press release, and it is important that these elements of format are followed. "Creativity" should be saved for the angle of the release, not its format. An improperly written release is irritating to the busy recipient and is more apt to find its way into the wastebasket than translating into print or electronic coverage for the retailer.

Two crucial format elements have already been covered—the "release date" and the "contact." These two format elements are always at the top of the press release. (Refer again to Figure 15.1.)

The overall aim of the rules that govern the format of the press release is to make the release easy to read and use. The release should be typed, double spaced, one side only, with margins wide enough to allow the editor to make notes or additions to the text for the printer.

Releases should be on standard white paper. This last rule does not preclude the use of special stationery for the press release. You will note in Figure 15.1 that Neiman Marcus uses a "cover sheet" or first sheet with a border containing the words "Media Information" on the top, and that all pages of the release bear the Neiman Marcus logo. The point here is that the release should use standard white 8 1/2- by 11-inch sheets and not be cluttered, as is often the case with stylized stationery.

About one-third of the way down on the first page is the headline. The headline should be centered, all caps, and either underlined or printed in bold. The headline should include an action verb and sum up the point of the release. When necessary, the headline may be followed by a subhead, which would further explain the purpose of the release.

Most press releases are limited to one page, however, there are instances when more than one page is required to tell the story. In the event the release runs for more than one page, there are format elements to indicate this and to help the recipient in the event the pages of the release get separated.

Purists call for the sender's name, address, and telephone number—placed top, left—on each succeeding page in the release. If you are using plain white paper, this is a rule to follow. You'll note that Neiman Marcus broke this rule; however, the store's logo on each succeeding page serves the same purpose.

One rule that is never broken in the multipage press release is the numbering of succeeding pages and the inclusion of a "slug line," which serves to identify the additional pages. In our example, *"add one—Neiman Marcus 1994 Christmas Book,"* indicates the second page of the press release regarding the same. Another approach, more commonly used, would have been *"Page two—1994 Christmas Book."* The slug line is important; the pile on the editor's desk could conceivably contain two or more press releases from Neiman Marcus, not to mention from other sources.

When the release contains more than one page, the accepted format style calls for "-more-" to be included at the bottom of each page. The end of the release, wherever it falls, is indicated by "###."

61 It took British jewelry designer Jonathan Ralston 850 hours to create his 18-karat yellow gold "Westminster Bear" studded with 200 diamonds, two cabochon sapphires, 36 cabochon rubies, and 20 cabochon emeralds. The quartz pocket watch chimes every hour. 6½" high overall. Available in the Precious Jewels Salon. For additional information, call (214) 573-5880.
61. "Westminster Bear," 200,000.00.

Figure 15.2

A time piece that is a conversation piece and a publicity grabber. Courtesy of Neiman Marcus.

Many press releases are written in straight news style. All the most important facts of the story are contained in the *lead paragraph* of the release. Each successive paragraph carries additional facts pertinent to the story in diminishing order of importance. This structure is referred to in journalism as the *inverted pyramid* form. Its major advantage is that it enables the reader—in this case the editor—to absorb all the facts from the start. If the editor has to search the release for scattered information, the release may be discarded.

When a publicist feels it is appropriate to the story, the release may be written in a feature news style. A feature news story adopts a more relaxed form, in which the facts unfold in the first and second paragraphs. The feature approach is less rigid than straight news style and is more entertaining.

Several factors must be taken into account when considering how Neiman Marcus bends the rules of the lead paragraph and the inverted pyramid form in its release. Given the news information contained in the Neiman Marcus press release—specifics about the gifts featured in the Christmas Book, and the fact that the store's Christmas catalog is famous, that is, the editor or program director is already aware that it contains unusual and exotic items—this was an effective approach. For the less famous, facts contained in the final paragraph of the release—where it was unveiled and that it is sent to 3 million customers worldwide—would best serve to capture attention if included in the first or second paragraphs.

Still, the lead paragraph in the Neiman release covers the meat of the release—the unveiling of the Christmas Book and the announcement of this year's "His and Hers" gift. The second paragraph is devoted to this perennial favorite.

Editors like quotes; they break up the story and lend weight to the point being made. The publicist can often find ways to take advantage of this fact. Note on page three of the release the proper way to accredit a statement. A major point that the publicist wanted to get across—that the book has something for everyone—comes across stronger as a quote from the company's CEO than it would have if the point had been made as part of the text. It also increases the chances of that important selling point being pick up by the media.

Contemporary news style is vigorous, simple, and direct. For the sake of clarity, the simple declarative sentence is favored, but not to the extent that the story becomes monotonous.

The wise publicity writer avoids inflated prose, superlatives (first, most, biggest, newest), and glowing adjectives. This "fluff" is the mark of an amateur and detracts from the news value of the release. Uncomplicated language and the simplest descriptions carry the greatest impact in print, which is, after all, the format of the press release.

DELIVERY

Depending on the topic of the press release, the publicist may decide that photographs or other support materials need to accompany the press release. Since

Figure 15.3
A perennial publicity favorite: the "His and Hers" gift. Courtesy of Neiman Marcus.

Figure 15.4
Press kit folder commonly used to send support materials with the press release.
Inside pockets hold 8 1/2- by 11-inch photos on the left, typed press release on the
right.

the Neiman Marcus release referred to the page numbers, it is clear that the
Christmas Book was sent with the press release.

The *press kit* (Figure 15.4) is a folder with inside pockets that organizes the
pages of the release, the photos, and any other pertinent material.

Summary

Publicity is a form of marketing communications used by retailers to promote the
store and its products. Unlike public relations, which uses a long-range plan to
create a favorable image for the store, publicity's function is to supply the media
with information about the store's various activities in order to get news coverage
for the store.

The publicity department gathers and selectively disseminates newsworthy
information to the various media through news releases. Often, press kits with

photographs or other visual material suitable for reproduction are used to deliver the press release.

By nature, publicity is unpaid-for exposure. What material is used therefore remains up to the discretion of the media. In this way publicity differs from advertising, which is conceived and designed by the store and placed in the media for a price.

The success of the publicity campaign hinges on the abilities of imaginative and skilled writers who are able to convey appropriate news to the appropriate sources.

Terms for Review

1. Publicity
2. News story
3. Feature story
4. Book
5. Public relations

6. Press release
7. Release date
8. Lead paragraph
9. Inverted pyramid
10. Press kit

Study Review Questions

1. What is the function of the publicity department?
2. What must a publicist consider when directing a news story to the editor of a particular publication?
3. The fashion publicist in retailing works with trade magazine editors, television producers, manufacturers' fashion coordinators, and in-store personnel. Why are these people important to the publicist?
4. What are the benefits of effective publicity?
5. Explain the term "inverted pyramid."
6. What approach does a straight news style take in a press release?
7. What approach does a feature news style take?
8. Which style would be appropriate to announce the appointment of a new store president?

Case

It is Anyplace Department Store's twenty-fifth anniversary. As the store's publicist, you have been hunting around for different angles on this news event. Some of the employees have been with the store since the first day it opened.

During the second year of operation, the store was the only building spared on Main Street when a fire swept the town.

Questions

1. What news story angles might you sell to the local TV station?
2. How would talking with the original employees help you do your job?
3. What approach would you use in a press release about the anniversary?

16

THE LAST LINK

The last and most important link in the sales promotion chain—the link that connects the store with its customers—is the sales staff. Meeting the customer face to face, the salesperson is the store's personal representative. All the money, time, and effort expended on the various aspects of sales promotion ride on the outcome of the encounter between the customer and the salesperson. The image the store has worked so hard to establish through its advertising, visual merchandising, public relations, and special events can easily crumble if the customer is met by an uninformed or apparently disinterested salesperson.

Role of the Selling Staff

Personal service is an important ingredient for customer satisfaction and in building customer loyalty for the store. The results of a survey, published in the November 1994 issue of *Consumer Reports,* emphasizes the important role the sales staff plays in the retailing industry. The survey respondents were most satisfied with retail stores that had the best sales help. Respondents rated the quality of merchandise for the price charged the second most important factor.

In addition to being the store's representative, the sales staff plays another—too often underutilized—role in the retailer's total sales promotion effort. This face-to-face encounter, between the salesperson and the customer, is one of the few opportunities the retailer has for two-way communication—for feedback from the target customer. Focus groups and advances in database marketing notwithstanding, the salesperson is in a position to conduct primary research for the retailer, to find out more about the customer's needs and preferences. Through its sales staff, the store has an opportunity to better understand and therefore more successfully target its customers.

Retailers who recognize their salespeople as important members of the store's team benefit in a number of ways. As with any organization, the retail employees who are satisfied with their employer have more loyalty toward the store and perform their jobs better. Since the customer's image of the store is formulated, in part, from contact with the store's salespeople, this is an important factor. If the store and its employees have a poor relationship, this will be telegraphed during the customer's dealings with the sales staff, and the retailer's image suffers.

Utilizing the sales staff to its full potential is just plain common business sense. After the cost of merchandise, employee costs—not just what the retailer pays in salaries, but increasingly expensive health care and other employee benefits—represent a large expenditure, which is worthy of careful attention.

Unfortunately, this important, final link in the sales promotion chain does not receive the attention it deserves. Too often customers encounter a salesperson who is unable to locate the advertised merchandise that brought the customer into the store, who does not have the selling information to help the customer make the purchase decision, and who is ill suited to represent the store to the customer. In this chapter we will examine some of the reasons why this situation exists, and some of the methods retailers use to combat the problem.

Today's salesperson is expected to do more than sell. As retailers tightened their overhead belts and eliminated support staff, duties such as cashiering, stock work, handling customer returns, and even wrapping have been added to the job description of the salesperson. All these duties can take away from the main function of the sales staff.

Some industry observers point to the absence of monetary incentives as part of the problem. The burden of paperwork created by the Fair Labor Standards Act, enacted in the mid-1950s, caused many retailers to drop commissions for their sales staffs. Except in select departments such as major appliances, women's shoes, or cosmetics, the industry norm was to compensate salespeople with a straight salary which in no way reflected their selling ability.

The makeup of store staffs has also drastically changed over the years. Industry experts estimate that only one-third of the approximately 16 million retail employees work year-round; the rest of the sales staff is classified as part-time help. In the majority of cases, these part-time employees are young people. Staffing a store with part-timers and young people creates a climate of high turnover and inexperience. To compound the problem, most stores have reduced floor supervision.

Some of the factors that have contributed to this situation are beyond a retailer's control. Years of widespread store expansion and extended shopping hours necessitated hiring part-time help. Because of their varied hours, part-timers as a group are more difficult to train, and high turnover makes the training battle a continuous one. Fewer people staffing a store has created the "floater syndrome" in which sales personnel are constantly reassigned to new areas, never getting the opportunity to learn the merchandise.

The net effect of all this is a drastic reduction in the art of personal selling and a weak last link in a store's promotional efforts.

But, as has been the theme throughout this book, retailers respond to customers' demands. It has become apparent that customers want and need better service, and successful retailers are giving that service to the customer.

According to *Consumer Reports,* a commission-driven pay system was responsible, in part, for the top-rating Nordstrom's sales staff received in its survey. Increasingly, top retailers are establishing some form of sales commission or reward system to motivate the selling staff and promote better service for their customers. Techniques such as working with each individual to agree on a "sales plan" and then rewarding the employee if the sales goal is reached or exceeded has proved successful for some retailers. Not only are sales increased, but the employee is included in the store's mission.

But providing the sales staff with an incentive to increase sales is only a piece of the total program at Nordstrom's. A company spokesperson declined to give specifics about the store's training program, which it considers proprietary, except to point to the company's philosophy—"Since 1901, Nordstrom has been guided by its founder's philosophy: offer the customer the best possible service, selection, quality and value."

Indeed, adherence to this philosophy permeates the organization; from the store operator to the executive staff, every encounter with the Nordstrom organization is service oriented. Some credit Nordstrom's beginnings, as a shoe store in Seattle—and the personal service associated with shoe salespeople, as the foundation of the organization's success. From the first Seattle shoe store, Nordstrom has grown into a specialty retailer offering a large selection of quality fashion apparel, shoes, and accessories for men, women, and children. The company fact sheet states that Nordstrom's merchandise ranges from contemporary classics to exclusive couture designs. With 77 stores in 14 states, Nordstrom's sales in 1993 were $3.6 billion. The company is scheduled to open 13 more stores through 1997.

Whatever the source, personal service has become part of the Nordstrom image, reputation, and company culture. It is widely recognized as the industry standard, prompting emulation.

Retailers employ various methods to project personalized service as part of the store's image and to change the customer's perception of the sales staff and the sales staff's perception of itself. In Figure 16.1, "Rich's is people who care" is an attempt to project the sales staff as an important part of the company's team, or in this case, the Rich's family. ("They've grown up with Rich's and become a part of our family....") The ad cleverly draws the reader in "...see if you can match the face with the way they were and the way they are." The copy under each employee's picture is designed to convey something about the person and the service they provide the customer. The ad helps "humanize" the store's staff for the reader (customer) and gives the employees recognition.

Other retailers have changed the name of the employee's function in the organization. Whether they are called "sales counselors," "sales associates," or something else, the point here is to elevate the role of the sales staff in their own

Figure 16.1
Rich's tells its customers (and its own people) that it cares about the store's employees. Courtesy of *Retail Ad Week* magazine.

minds as well as in the mind of the customer. Caution, however, must be the watchword in this approach; nothing is accomplished if the salesperson has not been, in fact, elevated in the organization.

Which brings us to the summary point in all the current efforts of retailers to strengthen the last link in the sales promotion effort. The selling staff has to be included, involved, "clued in." Training, both formal and informal, must be ongoing. If the sales "counselor" has not been given the proper "tools," that is, the appropriate information to perform as a counselor in selling the fashion merchandise, the retailer loses not only the potential sale, but the confidence of the customer and the employee.

A Profile of Personal Selling

There are a number of factors that constitute successful personal selling from both the store's and the customer's point of view. They include:

1. *Conveying selling points.* The salesperson should know enough about the merchandise to be able to talk about its major selling points. By pointing out its features, the salesperson gives the customer reasons to buy the merchandise.

2. *Closing the sale.* A successful salesperson senses when the customer needs additional reasons to buy the merchandise. Such logic as "This suit is a classic, you'll get several seasons out of it" helps motivate the customer to purchase.

3. *Encouraging patronage.* Through service, courtesy, and promptness, the effective salesperson makes the shopping experience a pleasant one, building customer loyalty for the store.

4. *Solving problems.* Service shouldn't end once the sale has been made. Helping to solve a problem for a returning customer is a vital aspect of personal selling.

5. *Suggesting additional merchandise.* Customers appreciate advice on accessory or companion merchandise. This facet of personal selling builds both customer loyalty and store profits.

6. *Retaining customer feedback.* Salespeople are the store's eyes and ears. To perform this function, they must listen carefully to what the customer is saying and forward the information to store management.

Retailers must convey to the sales staff that only by understanding the customer can the store and its staff meet that customer's needs—now and in the future. Successful sales personnel are trained to ask questions and listen to the answers to determine the customer's true needs.

Sales Training = Increased Confidence = Increased Sales

We all share a common human trait: no one likes to appear uninformed. Generally, salespeople welcome information they can pass along to the customer. The more information they possess, the more confident they feel. And confidence is contagious. When the salesperson is self-assured, the customer buys with confidence.

As we discussed earlier, today's retail environment presents difficulties in getting merchandise and sales promotion information to the sales staff, especially in large, multiunit retail operations. In a small store, information can be shared between the sales staff and the buyer or store owner through regular, informal meetings. Larger operations must take a more formalized approach. Employee fashion shows, merchandise reports or leaflets, films, slide shows, and videotapes are used to train salespeople and provide them with selling points about the merchandise. The main focus should be on customer benefits—this is the information that will make a sale and a loyal store client.

MORNING MEETINGS

Perhaps the most common, most efficient, and least expensive form of sales training is the *morning meeting.* Usually held a couple of times a week before the store opens, the meeting gives the sales staff and the buyer, owner, or department manager an opportunity for two-way communication.

Incoming merchandise should be discussed thoroughly. Samples are displayed as the group focuses on the major selling points and customer benefits. In a dress department, for instance, major topics would include:

- The basics
  - Name of manufacturer
  - Sizes available
  - Colors available
  - Fabric name, fiber content
  - How the garment should be cleaned
- Sales promotion information—where item is featured
  - Ads, when and in which advertising vehicle
  - Inclusion in the store's catalog, billing inserts
  - Visual merchandising—windows, store displays
  - Editorial credits in fashion magazines, newspapers
  - Other branches where the item can be found
- Fashion information
  - How the dress fits into the current fashion trend
  - Appropriate accessories—shoes, jewelry, and so on
  - Where the appropriate accessories are located in the store
  - Where the customer would wear the dress

- Benefits/selling points, for example,
  - Versatility
  - Ease of care
  - Packs without wrinkling, and so on

In addition, the discussion should focus on possible customer objections and how to overcome them. A revealing sundress, for instance, might warrant assurances that a strapless bra is the answer to that customer objection and that the store carries several styles to choose from.

The meeting is the opportunity for the salesperson to understand the reasons the item was chosen to be offered in the store. The thought process, from both the marketing and merchandising standpoints, is conveyed to the store representative who will have direct contact with the customer. Thus equipped, the "representative" is in a better position to make an individual sale. More important, the salesperson has the proper tools with which to perform his or her job—establishing a long-term relationship between the store and a satisfied customer.

The buyer, department manager, or store owner should use this opportunity to discuss customer attitudes, comments, objections, and requests with the staff, learning from their insights. Remember, this was called an opportunity for a two-way communication. The decision maker who does not elicit information from the sales staff is missing the opportunity to better know, and thus target, the store's customer.

Some procedure should be in place to ensure that the sales staff members not present at these information meetings are updated. Various methods include a typed information sheet or designating a person to conduct brief update meetings with part-timers or the evening shift.

OTHER EDUCATIONAL TOOLS

In addition to morning meetings, retailers use a variety of methods to educate the store's sales staff.

Employee fashion shows serve to convey selling information and increase employee enthusiasm for the merchandise that is being delivered to the store. Fashion shows are also a way for a store to show the employees how the "parts" fit into the "total" fashion picture and to promote interdepartment selling. Finally, the employee fashion show is a means of communicating to the store's employees their importance to the organization. It is an employee special event.

Occasionally, the sales staff needs more in-depth training to properly perform their jobs. *Merchandise seminars* are used to convey specific training information that cannot be covered in a meeting format. A merchandise seminar could be conducted before the store opens, or run during store hours, with the staff attending on a rotating basis. In some cases, attending a merchandise seminar is required before the salesperson is assigned to a particular department. This is common when the salesperson has to be able to perform certain functions or be specifically trained to properly serve the needs of the customer. The intimate-apparel depart-

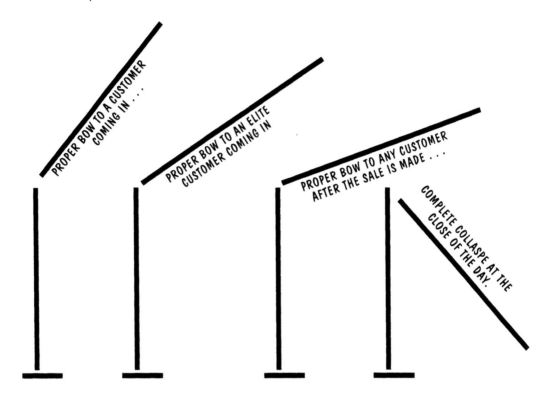

Figure 16.2

In the disciplined Japanese society, bowing is a way of life. Circumstances determine the degree of bow; a slight bend at the waist to the customer entering the store, a deeper bow to the elite customer than to the proletarian. To aid in training salespeople, stores in Japan use a bow-measuring machine. *Retail Ad Week* used this humorous sketch in an editorial calling for more training of salespeople in the United States. Courtesy of *Retail Ad Week* magazine.

ment, for instance, may require a new employee to attend a merchandise seminar to learn the proper way to fit foundations before assignment to the selling floor. Periodically, additional merchandise seminars addressing such topics as how to care for delicate fabrics, and what fashions or lifestyle developments have created the need for "special merchandise," would be used to update the sales staff.

Retailers similarly use training seminars to help correct problems the salesperson is having or just to continue the salesperson's "selling" education.

Manufacturers are particularly sensitive to the fact that the more information a salesperson has about a product, the more he or she sells. The manufacturer may schedule the designer or someone from the design staff to come into the store to talk with the retailer's sales staff. Many firms employ a *spokesperson* who travels across the country speaking to store staffs about the benefits of their product and selling points that should be conveyed to the customer. Some manufacturers use their own salespeople during off-peak periods to convey selling information to store personnel.

Another method that vendors use to educate the retail sales staff is to supply the store with literature or information packets. Videotapes and films are also used to set a mood of excitement about the merchandise and communicate important selling features. Vendor-sponsored fashion shows are another common device to educate and create excitement for the merchandise the store is carrying. When appropriate, the retailer should take advantage of these free training tools.

Summary

A vital link in a store's sales promotion program is the sales staff. Not only can an informed staff reinforce the image the store wishes to project, but a properly trained staff can be an important source of customer information, giving a retailer the opportunity for feedback from the customer it is targeting. While the modern retail environment makes staff training more complex, the retailer who meets the challenge will reap the rewards of higher profits, satisfied and loyal customers, and involved, enthusiastic employees.

Terms for Review

1. Morning meetings
2. Employee fashion shows
3. Merchandise seminars
4. Spokesperson

Study Review Questions

1. Explain how a salesperson can affect the retailer's sales promotion efforts.
2. Why does the sales staff represent the store's second highest cost of doing business?
3. Ideally, how should the retailer view the sales staff?
4. What factors go into successful personal selling?
5. How does sales training increase sales?
6. Give examples of the type of information the sales staff can supply management.
7. Why are merchandise seminars required for some departments?
8. How do the store's vendors participate in sales training?

Case

Anyplace Department Store has decided to take advantage of the heavy traffic on its main floor. It has set up a "theme boutique" to the left of the store's main entrance to showcase fashion merchandise. A "department manager" has been placed in charge of the boutique, and salespeople have been assigned there. The department manager chooses merchandise around a central theme from the various departments in the store. To create excitement, the merchandise in the theme boutique is changed regularly.

Questions

1. Describe the special training needs of the sales staff assigned to the theme boutique.
2. What types of information would the theme boutique salesperson need?
3. How often should training take place?

BIBLIOGRAPHY

Anderson, Leann. "Main Event; Staging an Event to Remember," *Entrepreneur,* Vol. 22 (November 1994), p. 148.

Book, Esther Wachs. "The Treachery of Success (Sally Frame Kasaks of Ann Taylor Stores Corp.)," *Forbes,* Vol. 154 (September 12, 1994), p. 88.

Cowan, Alison Leigh. "Judge Rules for Macy Parade," *The New York Times,* September 21, 1994, p. B1, Col. 2.

Cross, Richard, and Smith, Janet. *Customer Bonding: Pathway to Lasting Customer Loyalty.* Lincolnwood (Chicago): NTC Business Books, 1995.

Donahue, Tim. "Analysts, Customers Say That Nordstrom's Service Keeps Its Shoppers Loyal," *Gannett Suburban Newspapers,* March 12, 1995, p. 1E.

Downer, Stephen. "Getting Personal in Europe: Retailers Urged to Embrace Direct Marketing Techniques," *Advertising Age,* Vol. 65 (June 27, 1994), p. 12.

Drake, Mary Frances, Harrison Spoone, Janice, and Greenwald, Herbert. *Retail Fashion Promotion and Advertising.* New York: Macmillan Publishing Company, 1992.

Everett, Martin. "This One's Just for You (Direct Marketing Campaigns)," *Sales & Marketing Management,* Vol. 144 (June 1992), p. 119.

Fitzgerald, Kate. "Bloomies/Macy's Marriage Has Papers Sobbing," *Advertising Age,* Vol. 65 (July 18, 1994), p. 4.

"The Future of Shopping (Interactive Home-Based Shopping)," *The Economist,* Vol. 332 (August 20, 1994), p. 16.

Gitomer, Jeffrey. "Success Track (39.5 Selling Secrets)," *Entrepreneur,* Vol. 22 (March 1994), p. 158.

Grant, Linda. "Light at the End of the Tunnel; Federated's Move on Macy's Could Usher in a New Retailing Era," *U.S. News & World Report,* Vol. 116 (January 17, 1994), p. 59.

Grossman, Beth. "Meet the Press, How to Make Headlines," *Entrepreneur,* Vol. 22 (November 1994), p. 137.

Hofmeister, Sallie. "Fashion Ads Find the Great Outdoors," *The New York Times,* August 9, 1994, p. D1, Col. 1.

"Is There Gold in the Internet?" *The Economist,* Vol. 332 (September 10, 1994), p. 73.

Kim, Junu Bryan. "Databases Open Doors for Retailers: Precise Targeting of Shoppers Translates into Healthier Sales," *Advertising Age,* Vol. 64 (February 15, 1993), p. 38.

Mannix, Margaret. "Prizing Good Shoppers: Retailers Say Thanks with Discounts, Rebates and Gift Wrap," *U.S. News & World Report,* Vol. 116 (June 20, 1994), p. 74.

Morris, Bernadine. "The Joy of Shopping on Ladies Mile," *The New York Times,* February 17, 1995, p. C31.

Moukheiber, Zina. "Retailing (Industry Overview)," *Forbes,* Vol. 153 (January 3, 1994), p. 168.

Nachman, Barbara. "Not Just Another Pretty Face; Mannequins Reflect Changes in Fashion and in Life," *Gannett Suburban Newspapers,* March 6, 1995, p. 1C.

Piirto, Rebecca. "Catalogs with Byte (Home Shopping by Interactive Television, CD-ROM, and Online Services)," *American Demographics,* Vol. 16 (September 1994), p. 6.

"Retailers Invest in Multiple Technologies," *Computerworld,* Vol. 28 (June 27, 1994), p. 99.

"Today's Shopping Options," *Consumer Reports,* Vol. 59 (November 1994), p. 713.

Whittemore, Meg. "Survival Tactics for Retailers," *Nation's Business,* Vol. 81 (June 1993), p. 20.

Winters, Arthur A., and Goodman, Stanley. *Fashion Advertising and Promotion,* 6th ed. New York: Fairchild Publications, 1984.

GLOSSARY

Accrual The accumulated credit in a co-op program.

Adjacencies A consideration of visual merchandising; the effect of a display on a department next to it.

Ad layout The visual design of an ad.

Advertising plan Forecast of the advertising a store intends to use to reach planned sales goals.

Advertising ratio The percentage of the sales promotion appropriation allotted to the different merchandise classifications or areas of the store.

AIDA The acronym describing the fundamental tasks of any selling effort: attract *A*ttention, generate *I*nterest, create *D*esire, and obtain *A*ction.

AM frequency Amplitude modulation, a form of radio transmission that carries over long distances.

Anticipated annual sales What a company or retailer estimates the dollar amount of sales will be for a future year.

Art Visual component of an advertisement; its design and presentation.

Art director The coordinator responsible for the physical design and effectiveness of an ad.

Assortment ad Features more than one item; subclassified into omnibus, line promotion, related item, and departmentalized ads.

Audit bureau An independent business that checks and sometimes processes retailer co-op claims.

Bill-back In a co-op program, the amount the retailer bills the manufacturer.

Book An industry term for a magazine.

Broadcast media Television and radio.

Broadsheet Size of a newspaper six columns wide.

Broadside A type of self-mailer whose message continues as the piece is unfolded.

Business list Mailing list compiled from businesses' SIC codes.

Catalog Advertising medium in magazine format that illustrates and describes offered merchandise.

Chain A number of stores belonging to one company.

Clearance ad A sale ad used at the end of a retailing season.

Closed-back window A plate glass window in which the remaining three walls are enclosed.

Compiled list Mailing list collected from telephone books, club membership lists, and so on.

Comprehensive layout The ad layout containing copy text, headlines, and sub-heads.

Consumer The one who purchases—the ultimate customer.

Consumer magazine A general-interest magazine whose readers are consumers.

Co-op ad An ad paid for in part by someone other than the sponsor of the ad.

Copy The written message appearing in a print ad; the text or script of a broadcast commercial.

Copy block The written portion of a print ad that provides information to create interest in the merchandise or service offered.

Copywriter Person who writes the selling message of an ad.

Cost per thousand (CPM) The cost of reaching 1,000 homes or people.

Customer base People who repeatedly frequent the store.

Customer profile Facts about the typical customer who shops a store or department, such as marital status, income, age, and so on.

Database Information stored in a computer; databases enable the selection of names for targeted promotional efforts.

Database marketing Use of computerized records (databases) and the information that can be gleaned from them as a decision-making tool.

Demographics The statistical study of human population.

Departmentalized ad An assortment ad featuring a variety of merchandise from one department.

Direct advertising Advertising delivered to the prospect via mail, newspaper insert, salesperson, and so on.

Direct mail Advertising sent to the prospect through the postal service.

Discretionary income Money left over after the essentials are purchased.

Divisional advertising plan A detailed breakdown of the advertising plan for a department or division.

Duplication Reaching the same people more than once with an ad.

Employee fashion show A fashion show intended to convey selling information and enthusiasm to the sales staff.

External display Element of visual merchandising that includes the exterior of the building and window display.

Fashion event An event, taking various forms and accomplishing different goals, with fashion as its focus.

Feature story An article presenting news facts in an entertaining format.

Fixed line rate The amount the sponsor will pay for a line of newspaper advertising regardless of its actual cost.

Fixed percentage The percentage amount of net sales allotted to sales promotion.

Fixture Display unit that holds merchandise.

FM frequency Frequency-modulated or short-range radio that is static-free and of superior sound.

Focus groups A method of collecting primary marketing information; a representative group of the retailer's customers are invited to express their opinions on a variety of topics, enabling the retailer to have direct feedback from the store's customers.

Frame One-thirtieth of a second of a TV commercial.

Frequency Number of times a consumer audience is exposed to an advertisement.

Full-service advertising agency Firm staffed with highly skilled technical and creative people who specialize in selling, advertising, and marketing.

Good-neighbor ad An institutional ad designed to build the image of the store as a member of the community.

Growth area A department or classification of merchandise in a retail store that has an opportunity for increased sales volume.

Headline The featured idea of a print ad.

Home shopping Television programming dedicated to the presentation of items available for purchase. The customer now uses the telephone to place an order; the technology of interactive television will enable the customer to use the television to place an order.

House list A list of the advertiser's customers, likely charge customers.

Illustration The artwork of an ad; could be either line art or photograph.

Infomercial An extended commercial in a format that resembles regular programming.

Ingredient co-op Cooperative advertising payments to the retailer by producers of the ingredients that make up the final product, for example, fiber, fabric.

Institutional advertising Used to sell the organization; establishes and builds a reputation or image.

Institutional special event Event designed to create goodwill for the store.

Interactive shopping A range of electronic purchasing channels, including on-line computer networks and interactive television.

Interior display Visual merchandising inside the store.

Inverted pyramid A journalistic style in which succeeding paragraphs contain facts in diminishing order of importance.

Island window A display enclosed on all sides by glass.

Junior ready-to-wear Manufactured merchandise sold in retail stores and sized by odd numbers: 3, 5, 7, and so on.

Layout The format of an ad; the positioning of an ad's elements.

Lead paragraph The first and most important paragraph in a press release; contains the major point of the release.

Lifestyle What people are thinking and doing at a given point in time.

Line-promotion ad An assortment ad that presents the low end, middle, and top-of-the-line in a merchandise classification.

List affinity The appropriateness of the compiled list to the product offered, which thereby increases the chances of response.

List house Specialist service that collects, classifies, and sells mailing lists.

Local broadcast Broadcast sent from a local station.

Loss-leader ad A type of special-price ad in which profit margin is sacrificed to increase store traffic.

Mail-order advertising Method of advertising that prompts the customer to order merchandise through the mail.

Manufacturer co-op agreement The contract between the manufacturer and the retailer spelling out all eligibility requirements and limitations of a co-op program.

Marketing concept A retailer's merchandising and sales promotion programs formulated in response to external conditions rather than internal performance or manufacturer resource considerations.

Merchandise mix Items and products offered by a store.

Merchandise-related special event Event or activity designed to promote merchandise.

Merchandise seminar In-depth sales training which provides sales staff with particulars about the merchandise or specialized training.

Merchandising approach Consideration of internal store conditions and resources only.

Monthly department advertising budget A department's ad budget broken down by month to reflect historical sales fluctuation.

Morning meeting An efficient form of sales training which provides an opportunity for two-way communication between the sales staff and management.

National sales promotion Sales promotion conducted by the first two segments of the fashion industry, aimed at the ultimate consumer.

Net sales Gross sales minus reductions such as losses, customer returns, and so on.

Network broadcast A linkup of many stations allowing for simultaneous broadcast from one originating point.

Newsprint The quality of paper commonly used by newspapers.

News story A condensed article featuring only straight facts.

Omnibus ad An assortment ad that features merchandise from a variety of departments.

Open-back window A store window which has no back, providing an unobstructed view into the store.

Organizational chart A graphic which identifies responsibility, reporting lines, and communication flow within an organization.

Out-of-home advertising The advertising medium comprising transit advertising, billboards, phone kiosks, and the faces of buildings.

Partially open window An open-back window with either horizontal or vertical dividers which give the window definition while still providing a view of the store's interior.

Policy ad An institutional ad that conveys what the store stands for in terms of store services, hours, merchandise carried, and so on.

Postcard Form of direct mail requiring third-class postage.

Preferred position Spot in a newspaper where store would like ad placed.

Presell Creation of awareness and demand for a product at the consumer level.

Presentation The way a retailer distinguishes itself from its competition and communicates with its target customer.

Press kit Folder containing press release, photo, and other pertinent material.

Press proof The way the ad will appear in the newspaper.

Press release The vehicle used to send information or "news" to the media.

Prestige ad An institutional ad that addresses qualities that sets the store apart from the competition.

Price points The retail cost of merchandise carried or offered for sale.

Primary marketing data Marketing information generated by an organization for a specific purpose.

Prime time The hours between 7:30 and 11:00 P.M.

Production The division of an advertising department responsible for producing the end product.

Promotional ad Product advertising that promotes the selling of merchandise.

Psychographics Science of measuring and profiling consumer lifestyle traits, including interests, career mobility, and shopping patterns.

Publicity Media exposure that is not purchased, but is gained because it is "newsworthy."

Public relations A planned, long-term program to influence the public's image of the retailer.

Pull-through Process of sales promotion through which the producer or manufacturer of a product creates demand for a brand or product at the consumer level.

Push-through Process of sales promotion through which the retailer has the sole responsibility and control to create demand for a product at the consumer level.

Radio spot A 10-, 30-, or 60-second period of advertising.

Rate schedule The rates a medium charges for advertising time or space.

Reach The number of people in the defined target audience who will read, hear, or see the sales promotion message.

Regular-price ad Most common form of retail product advertising; ads featuring merchandise at regular price.

Related-item ad An assortment ad that features complementary merchandise from different departments.

Release date The date the information in a press release can be used.

Response list Mailing list made up of people who have previously responded to a direct-marketing offer.

Retail sales promotion Sales promotion conducted by the retailer which is aimed at the ultimate consumer.

Retailer-driven programs Extra funds supplied to the retailer by the vendor to use for special promotions; an extension of the regular co-op program.

Rough layout The first visualization or plan for an ad.

Run-of-paper (ROP) Ad placement that is left to the discretion of the newspaper publisher.

Sales letter A form of advertising or communication, usually customized with the recipient's name, in a letter format.

Sales promotion Communication, aimed at a prospective customer, with the objective to sell an idea, product, or service at a profit.

Sales promotion appropriation The amount of money a company spends on all its sales promotion activities.

Sales promotion calendar The retailer's sales promotion master plan.

Secondary marketing data Marketing information that already exists, for example, U.S. Census reports, private research studies, local newspaper readership profiles.

Self-mailer Direct-mail vehicle designed to be sent through the mail without an envelope.

Selling floor That part of the store where customers are allowed to go and where merchandise is displayed for them.

Shadow-box window A small, elevated, shallow window which provides maximum security.

Shifting demographics Changes in the population.

SIC code Standard Industrial Classification; codes businesses by industry.

Single-item ad An ad which concentrates on one unit of merchandise.

Special events Varied activities a retailer offers the public to add excitement, showmanship, and drama to the shopping experience; used to increase store traffic and sales and build or reinforce store image.

Special-price ad Offers merchandise for a less than normal price; used to build store traffic.

Spokesperson A person who represents the company in public.

Statement enclosure Direct-mail vehicle inserted into customer's bill.

Static ad A television ad, common on cable, which combines a still photo and text.

Store logo The retailer's business signature.

Store-wide event A special event in which the entire store participates.

Storyboard Artwork showing the sequence of a TV commercial.

Tabloid Size of a newspaper five columns wide.

Tearsheet A page torn from a publication to prove insertion of an ad.

Theme ad Draws its inspiration from a topical source other than the merchandise featured.

Tie-in Cooperation with or inspiration from an outside event or company.

Tonnage ad A single-item ad for merchandise intended to produce high-volume sales.

Trade sales promotion Sales promotional activities aimed at customers other than the ultimate consumer.

Traffic count The number of customers entering a store or department during a specific period of time.

Trunk show A type of fashion event in which the designer or manufacturer presents styles not available on the selling floor to the store's customers.

Type The printed letters in an ad.

Typeface The style of type and its size, measured in points.

Unified blend The coordination and mutual support of the various elements of the sales promotion and communication effort.

Vendor rate The cost quoted on a medium's rate card.

Vertical co-op Payment by the manufacturer to the retailer for co-op advertising featuring the manufacturer's product.

White space The portion of the printed ad left blank; an element of layout design.

Whole-firm advertising plan The advertising forecast for the entire store as well as the plans for individual departments or areas.

INDEX